*THE JOB
CONTENT
OF THE
U.S.
ECONOMY
1940–1970*

THE JOB CONTENT OF THE U.S. ECONOMY 1940–1970

JAMES G. SCOVILLE
Harvard University

McGRAW-HILL
BOOK COMPANY

New York
St. Louis
San Francisco
London
Sydney
Toronto
Mexico
Panama

*THE JOB CONTENT OF THE
U.S. ECONOMY, 1940–1970*

FOREWORD

This volume constitutes a significant exploratory study of long-term changes in the job content of the American economy. It has the merit of concentrating on the conceptual problems of defining occupations and job classifications, arranging them in a matrix to provide generality and design, and providing a schemata for measurement of change. The census data for 1940–1960 are reordered to reveal significant changes in the economy and are used as a basis for estimating projections for 1970.

In the day of the giant computer, the book calls attention to the gross inadequacies of our present census occupational data despite dedicated efforts to improve their quality. The 1970 census can provide only slight improvements. The attempt to describe the job complex of our modern industrial economy in less than 300 occupations, with one third of the work force falling into categories of "n.e.c." (not elsewhere classified) is one measure of our gross shortcoming. The very broad occupational categories often encompass job classifications with a great range and disparity in training and educational requirements and in wage levels, which distort significant analysis. The collection of occupational data by household interviews is a severe constraint on precision and detail. Moreover, occupational classifications which have their roots in a concern with socio-economic classes of society and a resolve that Marx did not apply to the new world are not an adequate basis for modern economic analysis. The analytical framework developed by Professor Scoville provides categories for the collection and organization of new occupational data and should provide a stimulus for an expansion in the systematic measurement of changes in job content.

Labor market policy and manpower planning require a considerable enlargement of our capacity to relate job classifications, and changes in their content quantitively, to a variety of significant economic variables in both the short and long run—employment, hours, education and training, seniority or duration of employment, age, compensation, turnover, and mobility.* The approach of this study also suggests a way of relating changes within an enterprise and those in the economy at large by the use of job families and levels of job content. While the present census data may provide a significant basis for the sociological study of social stratification and intergenerational mobility in the large, it is increasingly inadequate in concept and in measurement to the necessities and opportunities for the economic analysis of labor supply, compensation, and education or training by occupations.

Professor Scoville's analysis can also be fruitfully applied to the process of economic development. The changing occupational distribution of the southern states, in job family and job content level, over the years 1940–1970 is highly instructive. The author's comparison study of "The Job Content of the Canadian Economy, 1941, 1951, and 1961" (Dominion of Bureau of Statistics, Ottawa, Special Labour Force Study No. 3, April 1967) illustrates the value of comparative studies of occupational structures.

The volume should help to initiate a new and overdue interest in the measurement of occupational change and related economic dimensions of the economy and the enterprise. Students of manpower policy, industrial relations, and the economics of training and education will find the study imaginative and inspiring for further work.

John T. Dunlop

---

* See, the application of Professor Scoville's methods to the health manpower sector developed by Dr. Jeffrey H. Weiss, "A Job Classification Scheme for Health Manpower," *Health Services Research*, spring, 1968, pp. 48–64.

PREFACE

This study is a continuation and elaboration of the concepts and methods proposed in my doctoral dissertation. The refinements have generally been highly labor-intensive and thus extremely time-consuming. A principal advance from the earlier work has been the development of an experimental method for estimating levels of job content. This was no small task, but the reward, in terms of information about the characteristics of these occupations, was considerable. The research was financed in part through the program of The Manpower Administration, United States Department of Labor, under the authority of Title I of the Manpower Development and Training Act of 1962, as amended. Researchers undertaking such projects under government sponsorship are encouraged to express freely their professional judgment. Therefore, points of view or opinions stated in this document do not necessarily represent the official position or policy of the Department of Labor.

Although I bear full responsibility for errors of both omission and commission, the assistance and cooperation of many individuals was essential. Valuable comments and criticism have been made by many people—too numerous to list. However, special thanks are certainly due to John T. Dunlop of Harvard University. As the adviser of the original dissertation, he provided indispensable guidance and insight and has continued his active interest during the process of turning the initial work into a book.

The author is indebted to Joan Bloom, Michael Gaffin, and Robert Berliner for their conscientious labors in creating the detailed estimates, to Susan Tomkin and Joyce Smith for their patience in typing and retyping innumerable drafts, and to Virginia Sullivan for preparing the index. Finally, the long-suffering charity of my wife, Judy, cannot go unmentioned. Her assistance in the preparation of the earlier manuscript was invaluable, as has been her willingness to tolerate life with an economist.

James G. Scoville

CONTENTS

TABLES

Chapter 1

THE
PROBLEM
OF JOB
CONTENT

The vast number of jobs in our economy forms a highly complex structure. The underlying reality of millions of distinct jobs can be broken down in many ways to reveal particular characteristics of this structure. Jobs can be classified by industry, region, wage level, educational characteristics, age, sex, and race distributions, depending on the facets of the job structure under scrutiny. However, breakdowns of this type primarily describe characteristics of job-holders, and say very little about the jobs themselves. Although frequent mention will be made of educational, training, and wage distributions, all of which apply to workers, the central concern of this study is the content of the jobs in our economy. The principal questions which arise may be briefly stated.

1) What sorts of jobs are performed in the American economy—do people work with machines or tools, or money, or people, or papers and accounts? A framework of job content must reflect the major job foci—the technical processes, materials, or functions about which jobs are centered.

2) At what levels of relative job content are the various jobs performed? By job content we must clearly mean more than simple "skill," as the distinction between skilled and unskilled is applicable to only a small portion of the spectrum of jobs. Included in an assessment of job content must be consideration of responsibility and the range and complexity of duties.

3) To what degree are the abilities, skills, training, and other attributes which pertain to the various sectors of the job structure interchangeable? Where is the range of jobs which can be performed with a certain general set of abilities narrow or broad? How specialized or transferable are these abilities, skills, and training?

A number of uses can be advanced for a model and data classification constructed in the light of these questions. (See Chapter 2.) It will yield information about the process and results of technological change and market shifts. The approach should also be valuable in the analysis of projected changes in job content, with respect to the kinds and levels of education and training required, and possible changes in income or sex distributions. Such a framework should relate to the question of structural change in the economy, whether the pace is accelerating, and the directions in which we are traveling. An attempt is here made to develop an empirical description of the job content of the United States economy. The data as presently prepared are not especially suited to this purpose, so that the empirical work is necessarily experimental. Suggestions for the collection of more appropriate data will be a by-product of this study.

ECONOMISTS, DATA GATHERERS, AND JOB CONTENT

Changing distribution of employment among jobs, the emergence of new and the disappearance of old jobs are not new phenomena. Economists have long been concerned with the effects of capital accumulation and mechanization on employment and output, on wages and prices, and occasionally on changes in job structure and job content. As in any capsule history of thought, Adam Smith is our first landmark. For Smith, capital accumulation and division of labor are the driving forces of economic progress. One of the important aspects of division of labor is the increase in "dexterity" which accompanies it, but this has little bearing on the problem of job content as defined above (except as it arises from increased specialization). Smith does

introduce many of the factors involved in job content in a broad discussion
of the comparative requirements of agricultural and mechanical occupations.

> Not only the art of the farmer, the general direction of the operations of
> husbandry, but many inferior branches of country labour, require much more
> skill and experience than the greater part of mechanic trades. The man who
> works upon brass and iron, works with instruments and upon materials of
> which the temper is always the same, or very nearly the same. But the man
> who ploughs the ground with a team of horses or oxen, works with instru-
> ments of which the health, strength, and temper, are very different upon dif-
> ferent occasions. The condition of the materials which he works upon too is
> as variable as that of the instruments which he works with, and both require
> to be managed with much judgment and discretion. The common ploughman,
> though generally regarded as the pattern of stupidity and ignorance, is seldom
> defective in this judgment and discretion.[1]

Skill and experience, instruments and materials, judgment and discretion
—these factors serve to substantiate Smith's disagreement with the contemporary European practice which classed "mechanics, artificers, and manu-
facturers" as skilled, and country laborers as unskilled. It should come as no
surprise that very similar factors appeared above when the three questions
which served to focus attention on this problem of job content were posed.

Changes in the aggregate job content of an economy can arise not only
from the upgrading or downgrading of specific jobs, but also from shifts
in employment among various jobs. David Ricardo predicted such an effect on job content stemming from the accumulation of capital—although he
did not recognize it as such. Increased employment of machinery will dis-
place workers in circumstances where it involves reduction of the wages
fund, but will increase the "net income" of society. Increased profits from
this source, in conjunction with increased agricultural rents, will lead to
expanded employment of "menial servants." [2] It is clear that a shift from the
employment of craftsmen (displaced by the new machines) to employment
of such servants has the effect of reducing the level of job content in the
economy.

Karl Marx was probably the most voluble among economists in treatment of the impact of capital accumulation and technological change on the
nature of jobs. The process of mechanization and its various stages and the
effects of machinery in the hands of capitalists on the worker's life and skills
are discussed in *Capital* at great length and in great detail. Machines are

first contrived to do, with the same tools, that which men have done previously, with the man being "demoted to a source of motive power." Different sorts of machines are then applied to this problem, and man is supplanted as a power source. Not only is there a difference between tools and machines, but machines themselves are organized in two different fashions: large numbers of cooperating machines and "complex systems of machinery," wherein the continuity of the production process is imperative.[3] To Marx, the elimination of skills in the course of mechanization is clear:

> Along with the tool, the skill of the workman in handling it passes over to the machines . . . the technical foundation on which is based the division of labor in Manufacture, is swept away. Hence, in the place of the hierarchy of specialized workmen that characterises manufacture, there steps, in the automatic factory, a tendency to equalize and reduce to one and the same level every kind of work that has to be done by the minders of the machines.

Division of labor, which had under the system of "manufacture" (that is, craft industry) represented the specialized skills of workers, becomes in the factory primarily a distribution of workers among specialized machines.

In the production process itself, Marx distinguishes between workmen actually employed on the machines and engines (which drive the machines), and the "mere attendants" of these workmen. The latter, for example, include the "feeders" who supply the machine with material to be worked. In addition, there is a superior class of engineers and mechanics who look after the machinery. In a prophecy which history has not disproved, Marx foresaw the probable future use of machinery to replace the "mere attendants." He did not speculate as to whether the superior class of engineers and mechanics would grow accordingly.

Although Marx envisioned the elimination of the jobs of operatives and attendants, he emphasized that the process of capital accumulation led not only to the substitution of capital for labor, but of unskilled labor for skilled. The substitution of women and children for men is also a part of this general process. The over-all job content level of the economy tends to be lowered also by one further effect:

> At the same time that factory work exhausts the nervous system to the uttermost, it does away with the manysided play of the muscles and confiscates every atom of freedom, both in bodily and intellectual activity. The lightening of the labour, even, becomes a sort of torture, since the machine does not free the labourer from work, but deprives the work of all interest.

From this brief discussion, it is apparent that the factors which lie behind the content of individual jobs and the demand which the whole set of jobs makes on the labor force have received some recognition in the course of economic thought. Smith clearly outlined the major aspects of the job which affect its content, and Ricardo predicted changes in occupational structure because of the machinery which would impose lesser requirements on the skills and abilities of the work force. Marx combined these two factors to forecast changing content of particular industrial jobs along with shifts in the employment distribution from skilled crafts toward jobs with lower content. The treatment of this subject by economists, although sparse, has followed the lines of thought suggested at the outset of this work, emphasizing the determinants of job content and how they may change. In the sense that analysis has been directed toward it, existence of "the problem of job content" has been accepted in economic writing for almost two centuries.

Matters are different when we turn our attention to the development of American occupational statistics, and the problems which their developers sought to solve. Questions of job content, although raised occasionally, are not the object of inquiry with which data and classifications were concerned. Since the middle of the nineteenth century, under the guidance of occupational theorists and measurers like Francis Walker, Carroll Wright, William Hunt, and Alba Edwards, the basic data and their classification format have emphasized identification of the social and economic class structure of the United States.[4] Edwards summed up the goals of the census classification in 1943: the purpose of the social-economic groups is not to describe what jobs people perform, but covers a much broader scope.

> The occupations of a people influence directly their lives, their customs, their institutions—indeed, their very numbers. In fact, the social and economic status of a people is largely determined by the social and economic status of its gainful workers. And, were the figures available, the social and industrial history of a people might be traced more accurately through detailed statistics of the occupations of its gainful workers than through records of its wars, its territorial conquests, and its political struggles.[5]

In order to study this broad range of problems, Edwards declared:

> Occupational statistics, classified by major industrial divisions, are useful for showing in summary form the industrial distribution of the Nation's labor force. They are useful in the analysis of problems in which the workers are

considered merely or mainly as a productive force. But in the analysis of many of the problems which concern workers as people, and not merely as productive machines, as well as in the analysis of social and economic problems generally, there is, and long has been, a real need for statistics showing in summary form an occupational distribution of the Nation's labor force—a need for statistics that cut across industry lines and bring together into one occupationally homogeneous group all of the workers belonging to the same social-economic class, with but minor regard to the particular occupations they pursue or to the particular part of the industrial field in which they work.

The idea of making "work performed" the basis for occupational data is explicitly rejected in the above statement, and in the present census data. These data do not reflect the technical content of the job, either with regard to the principal equipment employed or major function performed. Instead, they were built up in view of sweeping questions of social status and progress. Clearly, major groupings developed in accordance with these principles will have little relevance to questions of type and level of work performed. The developers of the census scheme seemed to feel that an industrial breakdown of the labor force adequately covered this range of problems. Although the same broad job will differ in its detailed characteristics from industry to industry, it must be recognized that industrial classification is not a sufficient indication of the jobs people do. The social-economic groups do not reflect this goal either, and were not intended to do so.

A brief critique of the census occupational data may be in order. Since it is not their purpose, these data naturally do not reflect the several facets of job content; moreover, many of the social-economic groups and detailed occupations do not seem homogeneous as such. From the point of view of job performed or of social-economic status, the one-digit class known as sales workers cannot homogeneously contain insurance agents, stock brokers, newsboys, and hucksters. On the fine three-digit level, we could consider occupational group 335, "mail carriers," which is placed in the one-digit clerical group. In this case, one who uses the census breakdown is unwittingly counting as clerical workers post office truck drivers and chauffeurs. At another point, the lack of homogeneity is not even concealed by the title of occupational group 340—"officers, pilots, pursers, and engineers, ship."

These examples, which could be multiplied ad infinitum, demonstrate two criticisms of the present constitution of the data. First, jobs may be placed in incorrect categories on both the one- and three-digit levels, from either a "job performed" or a social-economic standpoint. In the second place, the categories may be so broadly defined as to remove all similarities among the various jobs. Although some parts of the classification show an explicit regard for skill differences, others do not. In general, the present scheme, especially at the one-digit breakdown into major social-economic groups, but also at the finer breaks, says too little about the similarities (and dissimilarities) of jobs, and almost nothing about skill or job-content levels.[6]

A second possible source of information about job content in the United States economy is the *Dictionary of Occupational Titles* (*D.O.T.*), although, if information is desired on the numerical importance of various types of jobs in our economy, it is necessary to look elsewhere. The purpose of the scheme used in the first and second editions of the *Dictionary* was to show the type of work done in various jobs; the new system of the third edition intends to correlate worker orientations and job characteristics more easily and thoroughly, but the goal remains the same.

> The United States Employment Service Dictionary is aimed . . . directly at the needs of the operating offices of the public employment service. It was thought of as a central device in a general program of furnishing information about occupations, with the more detailed job descriptions complementing it and adding supplemental information both about an industry as a whole and about its component occupations.[7]

The first dictionary was structured around an "occupational-industrial breakdown" of the labor force. This breakdown consisted of the following seven groups, shown with the initial digit of their code numbers:

0. Professional and managerial
1. Clerical and sales
2. Service
3. Agriculture
4. & 5. Skilled occupations
6. & 7. Semiskilled occupations
8. & 9. Unskilled occupations

The connection between this system of classification and that of the social-economic groups is fairly evident.

Over the years, a number of changes and additions have been made affecting the principles and content of the *Dictionary*. These are reflected in the third edition published in 1965. The first involved some reworking of the occupational-industrial breakdown; the second concerned the identification of 22 major "areas of work" which are further subdivided into "worker trait groups."

By far the most important development in the context of the present study is the attempt to measure the degree to which the jobs defined emphasize work with data, people, and things. The theory behind the distinction between data, people, and things was developed by Sidney Fine under the title of functional job analysis. "In the FJA method every job is conceived as requiring the worker to relate to three basic categories or primitives: Data, People, and Things." [8] The result is a framework involving "the use of a standardized language with which . . . to describe how workers function in jobs. The language used provides for an estimate of Level of function and Orientation, an estimate of relative involvement with Data, People, and Things." [9] Each of the three "primitives" is described by a hierarchy of eight action verbs which define the relationship of the worker to data, people, and things in terms of what he does to or with them. "These functions [that is, the action verbs]—which identify levels of activity—can be used equally well to define and describe what all people do regardless of the particular content of the job." [10]

It is not self-evident that the levels of involvement with data, people, and things are the relevant job characteristics for a wide range of questions. The concept that the method fully or satisfactorily "describes how workers function in a job" depends on the sense of the word "function." The important psychological or placement aspect may well be how a person relates to certain salient features of his job. An economic or technological standpoint, however, will require a different definition. Without denying that specific jobs may demand specific outlooks, orientation, and character traits, training requirements, wage structure, and worker mobility may have very little to do with the data, people, and things relationships per se. Rather they will depend upon the manner in which these parts are organized by the particular technology.

Some of these comments can best be made in view of the concept of job focus or family. Training requirements, not only in terms of time but of their actual content, are clearly dependent upon the specific technology, materials, or functions about which the family is centered. The wage structure of the economy depends on groupings of jobs among and within industries and job families. Worker mobility depends on a wider range of economic and social factors; even actual worker movements from job to job may be dominated by movements along the promotion ladders of job families.

From a technological point of view, identification of absolute and relative levels of relationship to data, people, and things may say very little about what the worker really does in the job. Thus, the following jobs, drawn from a longer list, have identical levels of involvement with the three primitives of functional job analysis: university registrar, park ranger, coroner, taxicab starter, and head chef. Such a grouping suppresses important information about the technical focus of the job, about patterns of promotion and nature of training—that is, fails to yield comprehensible information about the level of job content. In general, it seems that we must take exception to the conclusion that functional job analysis allows us to "define and describe what all people do regardless of the particular content of the job."

CONCLUSION

The nature and determinants of job content and the impact thereon of economic and technical change have a long established (if low priority) place in the annals of economic thought. In particular, Adam Smith clearly and forcefully observed some factors and circumstances which make the content of one job differ from that of another. I contend that job content has two principal dimensions—the means and functions on which jobs focus, and the level of content with regard to skills, responsibility, and complexity of duties generally.

In contrast to economists' perceptions on the determinants of job content, U.S. data on occupations, as prepared by the Census Bureau, have looked to the economic and social strata of society. It must in fairness be concluded that economists as well have dwelt more on the latter problem than the former.

The census data meet criticism on three grounds. The present statistics were not designed (and are not particularly useful) to answer the three questions posed about jobs and their content; the distribution of the detailed data among the major social-economic groups is weak and inconsistent; the basic detailed figures themselves are very weak. The first criticism is not, independent of the others, an argument that the existing data are inapplicable to the range of problems for which Hunt and Edwards designed them. However, today we recognize a different set of questions and problems which demand analysis. It is in the light of job focus and job content that a new scheme must be constructed, not with a view to the social and economic status of occupations.

The Dictionary of Occupational Titles cannot be used to estimate the job content of the American economy because employment data are not associated with the titles. Furthermore, there are serious conceptual and operational difficulties with the data, people, and things hierarchies which are used in the 1965 edition of the *Dictionary*. Measurement of involvement with data, people, and things was undertaken originally for its value in placement; the transferability of this concept to other problems is unclear. This method ignores the contributions of the particular technical, functional, or material focus at the content of the job. Its relevance to economic and technological questions of training, wage structure, and worker movement may therefore be sharply limited.

Chapter 2

JOB CONTENT AND THE RECLASSIFICATION OF OCCUPATIONS

To construct an informative scheme of occupational classification, an appropriate model of the job content of the economy is required. Given the structure and nature of the capital stock, technology, product and factor markets affecting use of resources, and the levels of education and training, the various types of jobs which will exist are substantially determined. Changes in the amount or nature of cooperating capital will alter the content and number of associated jobs and thus affect their qualitative nature and quantitative distribution in the economy. Similarly, changes in the manner in which capital and labor are utilized will affect content. For example, as workers become more familiar with tools and equipment, they alter the methods of work and the distribution of skills involved. In view of the changing nature of jobs in our economy and some of the intrinsic features and interrelationships of jobs themselves, a useful and proper subdivision of the whole spectrum of jobs in the economy will be developed with this object: to reflect the job content of the American economy in order to assess it at a point in time, and analyze its patterns of change over time.

THE DIMENSIONS OF JOB CONTENT

In the analysis of the work performed in our economy, two primary questions arise. First, what types of jobs are being done; second, what are the relative amounts of skills and abilities which characterize the various jobs? These basic questions identify the two major aspects which the job-content model seeks to describe. Job content is thus conceived to have two main dimensions: the job family and the level of job content.[1]

A job family is defined by the material, equipment, or functions about which the jobs in it are centered. In any discussion of job content, it is crucial to determine the focus of the job. The content of the job depends on a number of factors about which one can ask this type of question: does the job involve handling materials, tools, machines, money, or dealing with people? The importance of such technical conditions has been treated by John T. Dunlop,[2] and requires little discussion at this point. Such considerations determine in large degree the required skills, effort, and responsibilities. The technical dimension influences both the level and the distribution of the job requirements, and is often related to mobility and to relative wage structure. Jobs with a similar focus—involved with the same general work—will be grouped into job families by this major focus.

On the aggregate level, these job families are the analogue of the families and clusters which have been discussed by Dunlop and E. Robert Livernash on the plant level.[3] They form the basic fabric for the structure of jobs in an industrial economy. Dunlop has defined a job cluster in these terms:

> [It] is a stable group of job classifications or work assignments within a firm (wage determining unit) which are so linked together (a) by technology, (b) by the administrative organization of the productive process, including policies of transfer and promotion, or (c) by social custom that they have common wage-making characteristics.[4]

These clusters are important in the movement of labor into, through, and from the plant, and in relation to the wage structure. Livernash has suggested several broad types of job clusters: (a) the "departmental function group," where promotion and wage patterns are connected with departments or divisions of a firm; (b) skill families, (c) related types of work, and (d) the "work crew or closely knit work group."[5] The common technological and promotional focus of various jobs (important on the plant level) will be the major unifying factor for the identification of job families for the economy as a whole.

The second principal dimension of job content concerns the levels of complexity within the various job families, and comparison of job content among families. The technical aspect of job content is covered by the division of the job structure into families; the content-level breakdown will relate to all the factors which affect the complexity of the job. As has long been recognized, the narrow concept of skill is inadequate to describe the content of most jobs. The level of content depends not only on manual dexterity, but on the mental function, as well as responsibility and coordinating duties. In accordance with the relative range of duties, skills, and abilities involved, jobs should be ranked within the job families, just as they are ranked in actual job-evaluation systems. Such a twofold breakdown will indicate for the whole economy the major technical foci of jobs as well as the relative levels of content.

Other factors undoubtedly affect the content of the job in important ways. The same general type of job will vary across industry lines, as the technical conditions are altered and the kinds of work are changed. Thus, "blasters and powdermen" in the census include both workers at a mine face and those who blast stumps from fields. There is a genuine difference in job content arising from variations in equipment and techniques employed. Similarly, differences in content can arise within a broad type of job because of geographical factors. Farming is a clear case in point, where techniques, crops, and equipment vary considerably from region to region. In theory then, a complete enumeration of jobs would involve a greater subdivision into job families and content levels. However, within the range of our ability to construct homogeneous job families, such regional and industrial variations should be relatively unimportant.

This approach to the jobs in an economy conceives their important dimensions to be the technical aspect of what is done, and the level of content at which it is done. It should be stressed that a system of data based on this model will yield information not available in the present social-economic or industrial breakdowns. The social-economic groups describe large groups of the work force in terms of their social and economic status. These data make little attempt to describe types of jobs performed in terms of technical orientation, and yield only limited information with regard to levels of content. Similar criticism can be directed against the industrial breakdown of the labor force. This breakdown focuses on the end product of the process in which a job is incorporated and does not reveal the particular type of function performed or service rendered. To reveal the nature and content of the jobs in the economy, a new system is required.

There are three principal uses which can be advanced for such a model of job content and which serve as reasons for its development. In the first place, knowledge of the relevant aspects of job structure will provide a useful framework for the study of wage structure. Some changes in the wage structure of the economy will derive from changes in content. Similarly, the job families have attributes which are important for a discussion of wage determination. Thus the scheme of job content may be useful in the analysis of wage changes which may accompany changing patterns of employment.

In the second place, the identification of types of jobs performed and the levels of skills, abilities, and training will be useful in the analysis of mobility, actual and required. Mobility varies generally with the level of content, and it should be possible to study the mobility of workers from one job family to another and between various job-content levels. Such knowledge is relevant to the study of the operation and responsiveness of the labor markets involved.

Finally, the creation of a system to summarize the technical foci of jobs and the various levels of content will be useful in analyzing training and educational requirements. As the structure of demand for goods and services changes, so will the associated job content. In addition, technological change will affect some sectors of the job structure more than others. In the framework of content, projected changes in markets and technology can be linked to the changes in the kind and level of training required.

These purposes and goals can be briefly contrasted with those of the social-economic groups. The latter were initially intended to reflect the "station of labor" and to reveal its rise on the "social scale of life." The social-economic groups were explicitly designed by Alba Edwards not to reflect primarily either occupation or industry, but social class. In contrast, the purpose of this study is to identify the kinds and complexity of the jobs performed in our economy and to propose an experimental measure of these dimensions of the job structure.

JOB STRUCTURE AND THE PRINCIPLES OF CLASSIFICATION

When jobs are structured by the types of work performed and the levels of job content, they will display certain other interrelationships, arising from market and technological factors which are important from the viewpoints of mobility, training, and wage structure. We identify the interrelationships briefly as promotion, substitutability, and transferability. They underlie the basic homogeneity which permits use of the concept of a job family and are important characteristics of the various levels of job content. As these factors are important in the theoretical analysis of content, they must also affect attempts to produce an empirical classification.

Promotion. There exist in the job structure, just as in a single plant or operation, ladders of promotion from the bottom of a relevant group to its top. The ladders through the job structure pass through both internal and external labor markets, and thus are less rigid and defined than those within the firm or operation. Thus, employees advance not only through the internal labor market of the firm, but also by passing from firm to firm and industry to industry.

The rungs on these ladders are usually associated with differences in required skills, abilities, and responsibilities. Generally there are well-established lines of promotion between various jobs, and the levels of content follow these lines, whether they pass through the plant or through the external labor market. These ladders are commonly linked with layoff and transfer patterns for the particular plant or unit of operation and are also related to problems of wage structure.

The first step below a job, in terms both of promotion and of content, is often one of "assistant" or "helper." Machinists' helpers generally provide materials, clean up the workplace, and perform lower-skilled jobs to expedite the work of the craftsman. Usually, the focus of a helper's job is the same as that of the man he helps, being involved with the same materials, equipment, and processes. Numerous cases could be cited of job clusters about large industrial machines: for example, the melters' and helpers' jobs associated with an open hearth, ranging from the foreman to the cinder pitman. Similar is the hierarchy of jobs found in a rolling mill—with the roller at the top, next, his assistant, and then the jobs of finisher, speed operator, and rollhand, among others. A further example of a promotion ladder is found on the railroads, where new operating employees are generally hired as firemen or brakemen and are promoted to engineers and conductors. These groupings and ladders are exemplary of the job family on the micro-economic level of the operating unit. The job families which are identified in the economy as a whole should also contain broad avenues of promotion: a common technical focus will characterize jobs at different levels of the promotion ladder.

Transferability. This denotes the ability of a man with certain fairly standardized skills and abilities to perform a range of different jobs. Thus a skilled electrician (perhaps in part due to the broadness of the term) is competent to do many jobs of very different natures, and in many different manufacturing industries, as well as in construction and maintenance. Similarly, a "machinist" who stands in the earlier craft traditions of the IAM must be able to work on a wide variety of machines. Typographers, during apprenticeship, are required to master a certain number of methods and techniques employed in the printing trades. The existence of transferability among the members of the labor force, and the scope of it, are relevant to problems associated with changes in structure.

Substitutability. For some jobs, there exists a range of "occupations," reported in the census of population, which satisfies the various skill, ability, and training requirements of the job. Depending on various circumstances (for example, the level of aggregate demand), the types and levels of skills and abilities brought to the job will vary. In part, this may reflect a loosening of requirements—the sort of thing that Melvin Reder claimed to observe over the business cycle,[6] and which Wesley C. Mitchell saw as the source of some cost increases in prosperous times.[7] Richard A. Lester has analyzed a tight labor market during the Korean War and concluded that the reduction of hiring standards was an important method of relieving shortages.[8] In other cases, by a reorganization of the work pattern, different sets of qualifications may be accommodated to the job. For example, the extreme short-run necessity of obtaining substitute teachers can lead to different requirements, while various clerical and administrative facets of the job may be waived. An opposite case would exist in the use of overqualified personnel, such as that noted by Walter W. Heller in the underemployment of professional workers in times of general economic slack.[9] Substitutability is in some respects on the same side of the coin with transferability, but refers to the range of persons who can perform a job, while transferability refers to the range of jobs that a person can perform. Both are logically opposed to the narrower ranges of movement implied by the concept of specialization.

The three characteristics just examined refer, either in terms of the technical focus of the job or with respect to the dimension of content level, to the relations among the various jobs found in the economy. When developing the actual reclassification of existing data, these characteristics must be kept in mind. The job families developed will depend on the characteristics of promotion and assistance in the employment of various materials or equipment, or the performance of services. The breadth of the families will depend on the substitutability and transferability of the included occupations.

THE RATIONALE OF THE JOB FAMILIES EMPLOYED

Starting from the grossest aggregate—total employment—this study attempts to devise an experimental system of subclassification which will display the major job families in the American economy. A successful classification is rather like an accordion—capable of being meaningfully expanded or contracted. Ideally, there may be no reason to stop the expansion short of the point where even the individual's idiosyncratic contribution to the particular job is described, but in reality one must stop a good distance before such fine detail is achieved. The broadness of the census occupational data per se will require that the job families also be fairly broad. In general, the utility of the job family breakdown will depend on the balance between the information to be gained and the ability of the economist or his data to discriminate between job families.

A first attempt at division of job structure into families might parallel the present social-economic distinction between blue-collar and white-collar jobs. However, many types of service occupations are not adequately covered by such a simple division and must be recognized as a separate broad field. In addition, farmers do not fit conveniently into either a white-collar or a blue-collar group (as these terms are normally used), so that our information is increased by classifying them separately. Four principal regions of the job structure can serve as the starting point: blue-collar, farm, white-collar, and service. In this attempt to quantify job structure by technical or functional content, the following job families will be identified. Within blue-collar jobs, families are found focused on tools, machines, the operation of vehicles, and inspection and supervision. The broad range of white-collar and service jobs can be broken down by the following major foci: sales, clerical, personal services, entertainment, protection, education, health services, welfare services, administrative jobs, and jobs in research and design.

The method employed is necessitated by the nature of the detailed data, which apply only to major occupations or groups of them. This requires a deduction of useful job families from the total range of employment and as accurate an application of the data as is possible. If sufficient data existed to identify the job clusters and families within individual units of operation, then they could be aggregated to yield the job families of the economy as a whole. However, the form of the data at present requires the use of a more deductive approach to job families.

In considering the range of industrial blue-collar jobs, more information about content is obtained by a distinction based on the size and complexity of the capital goods associated with the job. The skills, abilities, and responsibilities depend on the size of capital goods, the complexity of possible operations, and (to some degree) the number of people associated with the job. Differentiation will be made within the general blue-collar area between jobs focused on "tools" and jobs focused on "machines and equipment." The "tools" focus covers jobs which range from the use of the simplest tools—the shovel, pick, and mattox of a ditchdigger—through the more complex tools employed by various mechanics, up to the smaller machines for which a single man is responsible, as in the job of a compositor. Within the "machine and equipment" focus, we place the operators and attendants of large machines, often those which are incorporated into a longer, continuous process of production such as an assembly line. In an assembly line, a man may use a very simple tool, but the focus of his job comes within the realm of the whole machine.[10]

A certain class of machines and equipment which differs in general job focus and content from the others comes to mind immediately—the various vehicles. Hence, we place in a separate "vehicle operation" family the operators of motor vehicles and trains and some of their associated workers.

Within the general area of jobs concerned with the application of tools and machinery to the production of goods, there exists another distinct and separable group of jobs. This is composed of those who supervise the work, generally checking both the performance in the workplace and the quality of the resulting goods. For lack of a better term, this will be denoted the "inspection" job family. Because of the similarity of the methods of testing the quality of goods, both those involved in inspection on the production line and those independently engaged in the checking of product quality will be included in this family. It should be noted that, in this case, the functional characteristics of a set of jobs have been allowed to override the promotion ladder criteria.

Within the "tool" and "machine and equipment" job families, a further breakdown can be performed, in light of the question posed earlier about the specialization of various jobs. It was mentioned that transferability and substitutability are both opposed to specialization. A distinction will be made between specialized and nonspecialized jobs. This distinction is relevant in type and direction of training and the interjob and interindustry mobility of workers.

It is evident that many families within the structure are specialized by their very nature. Occupations within health services tend to be highly specialized, and education tends perhaps to be less specialized. On the other hand, some selling jobs, where the same general abilities and training are applicable in many areas, are clearly nonspecialized. Ideally, the concept of specialization could be applied to all families in the job structure. However, the area in which the distinction will in practice yield the most information with respect to training and mobility is in the tool and machine and equipment job families.

In brief, specialized jobs have narrower ranges of content and industrial applicability than do nonspecialized jobs. In the first place, specialized occupations tend to have low levels of transferability; the occupation only covers a narrow range of differing subjobs. Also, specialized jobs are not characterized by substitutability in the type of worker who can perform them. Specialized jobs have a narrow range of technical content which is associated with a highly specific collection of required skills and abilities. Specialized jobs will also tend to have a low degree of inter-industrial applicability, while nonspecialized jobs will remain more or less constant in job content from industry to industry, and will be found in many industries.

Thus, an attempt is made to determine the occupations which have a narrow and unified range of duties and job content, which are related to narrow and specific employment requirements, and which are not applicable to a wide range of industries or products. We call such occupations specialized, and those of fairly broad content and applicability, nonspecialized.

Two other matters arise on which present problems and developments have focused attention, but which cannot be reflected in the matrix of job content. In the first place, content will differ between jobs centered on the direction of a machine and jobs simply tending (or adjunct to) a machine. This distinction is largely irrelevant to the tool family as we have defined it, if the jobs involved are largely individual. But in the machine and equipment job focus, such a division would be extremely important because of technical change. The growth of mass production created a great number of jobs for those who cooperate with a large amount of complexly organized capital. Any assembly line of the classic sort called for large numbers of adjunct workers. The question of whether this structure is changing is frequently raised in economic literature. It is easy to find specific cases, but we have no measure yet of the over-all impact on the two job types. Along with this problem are questions about the extent to which jobs involving the direction of large machines are being created, and the character and direction of change in skills and job content involved in other classes.

A parallel problem in the present American situation concerns the balance between production jobs and maintenance jobs—in this case among jobs in the tool family. With the relative growth of all kinds of services, especially if a sharp decline in the jobs adjunct to large machines is to be expected, the structure of tool jobs in maintenance functions becomes very important. The types of skills involved in our economy will depend in part on the relative changes in these two job classes. Whether "automation" raises or lowers the skill-mix of the economy cannot be known unless we can measure the shifts from production to maintenance jobs, and from jobs cooperating with large machines to jobs directing them, the impact on jobs outside the plant, and various related aspects of job content. Unfortunately, to make empirical distinctions based on those of theory would put too much strain on the present occupational data. The data simply do not reflect these distinctions sufficiently to allow the derivation of useful information.

The broad farm group is logically capable of further subdivision. A clear difference in promotional patterns exists if the operator is an owner rather than a tenant or employee. The data of the agricultural census also indicate differences in job content—owner-operated farms are larger, have greater investments in buildings and equipment, and hire more workers.[11] Unfortunately, the population census classifies owners and tenants together, and hence we shall distinguish only one farming job family.

The classifications so far discussed, when applied to the existing occupational data, cover roughly 25 million workers in a total employment of 61 million in 1960. The broad range of service workers and white-collar workers remains to be classified—approximately 36 million workers in all. Without any rigorous attempt to defend the number of additional job families chosen, I shall briefly discuss each of the ten families used to complete the system. It appears, when balanced against the quality of the existing data, that these families yield as much information as possible.

Sales. Within this classification, composed of those whose principal job focus is the sale or purchase of goods and services, two subfamilies will be distinguished. One flaw of the present census sales-worker category is its lack of homogeneity. There is, for instance, a big difference in workers who know the product and its characteristics (stockbrokers, for example) and workers whose jobs require little if any knowledge beyond that of the availability of a narrow range of products and prices (newsboys). To some extent, this family subdivision will reflect important differences in the level of job content as well. It is related to the specialized–nonspecialized distinction recognized in the tool and machine and equipment job families. (In all tables, sales jobs requiring considerable knowledge of product characteristics will be denoted by Sales A; the other jobs by Sales B.)

Clerical. This includes jobs largely responsible for the creation and keeping of records, correspondence, and the like—pretty much the same as the present clerical classification in the census. It includes some sales jobs where the keeping of records is more important than the sales aspect (for example, ticket and station agents), and some jobs adjunct to normal clerical work, particularly messengers. In the future, the data might be constructed to reflect the differences between jobs involved with very simple office machines and the newer data-processing jobs associated with electronic equipment.

Personal service. These jobs may or may not include the use of various types of tools and equipment, but are principally focused upon providing service to a customer (barbers) or groups of customers (elevator operators). Also included are private household workers, maids, cooks, and equivalent occupations.

Entertainment. This includes the performing arts as well as associated service workers (ushers). The nature of the census data forces us to include music and dancing teachers, and this is not entirely inappropriate.

Protection. This is a fairly self-explanatory family, encompassing fire and police protection occupations.

Education and training. This includes all types of teaching jobs, except in the performing arts where the entertainment aspect was judged more important than the teaching function. Also included are the various types of industrial-training instructors included by the census in "teachers, not elsewhere classified."

Health services. This is a broad family, including jobs in the general area of health and related services. Many are characterized by similar procedures for training and preparation.

Welfare services. Both spiritual and social welfare occupations are included in this job family. A purist might distinguish between them, but the broad range of tasks performed roughly coincides.

Administration and organization. This family includes jobs whose primary focus is the administration of an enterprise, office, or firm, or those jobs which are part of the administrative framework of the government (judges and public officials). Most entrepreneurs are in this family; theoretically they should be segregated. However, the existing occupational group, "managers, officials, and proprietors, not elsewhere classified," neither includes all entrepreneurs, nor is made up solely of entrepreneurs. Thus a separate empirical family to follow the distinctions of theory seems unwise.

Research and design. This family might also in theory be further subdivided, but in fact the distinction is hard to make. Natural and social scientists, technical engineers, and various types of design workers are included.

At this point, a recapitulation of the job families devised may be useful. This is done in Table 1 with the numbers employed in 1960 shown to give an idea of relative size. The figures were built up from the detailed occupational data of the census in accordance with the allocation of census occupations to job families shown in Appendix I.

Table 1. Job families and 1960 employment.
(millions)

Job family	Employment
Total	61.5
Tools	
specialized	2.4
nonspecialized	9.3
Machines and equipment	
specialized	1.0
nonspecialized	7.4
Inspection	1.7
Vehicle operation	3.1
Farming	4.0
Sales	
considerable knowledge of product[a]	1.3
little knowledge of product[b]	4.0
Clerical	9.5
Personal services	5.4
Entertainment	0.4
Protection	0.7
Education and training	1.9
Health services	2.0
Welfare services	0.4
Administration & organization	5.6
Research & design	1.4

[a] Hereafter referred to as Sales A.
[b] Hereafter referred to as Sales B.

THE RATIONALE OF JOB-CONTENT LEVELS

The second basic problem to be confronted by a classification scheme designed to reflect job content concerns the levels at which jobs are ranked within the job families. The job-family dimension has yielded information about the technical directions in which jobs are oriented, but one still wants to know about the levels of skills, abilities, and training required. The question of skills or skill levels, their definition and measurement, is unfortunately yet unanswered. There is no automatic method which can be drawn from the literature and applied. Nevertheless, the problem confronts us—how can an appropriate system of job evaluation be set up within the job families previously established?

This primary problem is complicated by a second—can content levels be defined within job families which are in some way comparable so that they can be summed across job families? Not only is a relative vertical ranking of jobs desired, but horizontal comparability is needed if the over-all job-content composition of the economy is to be studied.

A sizable literature exists on the purpose and methods of job evaluation, although not usually on an economy-wide basis. An exception to this is found in the Netherlands where a nationwide "Normalizing Method" of job evaluation was used in wage policy. The purposes and weighting factors involved are much the same as those for a plant or industry.[12] A recent publication of the International Labor Office has stated:

> Job evaluation may be defined simply as an attempt to determine and compare the demands which the normal performance of particular jobs makes on normal workers without taking account of the individual abilities or performance of the workers concerned.[13]

This, in general, is also what the content-level dimension of a job-content matrix should represent. The publication just cited summarizes an international sample of job-evaluation plans and notes their many common features. A typical plan is that for the American steel industry which is based on twelve major facets of job content: pre-employment training; employment training and experience; mental skill; manual skill; responsibility for materials; responsibility for tools and equipment; responsibility for operations; responsibility for the safety of others; mental effort; physical effort; the surroundings of the job; and hazards of the job.[14] Once the job-family breakdown has been established, these are the typical criteria for ranking jobs within the focus-oriented families.

Considerable information exists on job content and requirements, but very little to allow a comparison of the entire grouping of jobs in the economy. The vast preponderance of job content data is to be found in job-evaluation or description manuals of various companies or industries. Needless to say, comparability among such sets of job descriptions was not the goal of the producers of the manuals. Furthermore, wide ranges of the economy are not included in such studies, with the professions and service trades the most obvious examples. Even when the number of "jobs" surveyed is restricted to those in the census, most of the information has no direct connection with content. The census publishes occupational characteristics like age, income, educational distributions, racial, regional, and sex breakdowns, and even marital status. There are, however, no data on the content or requirements of these census groups.

The only attempt to study a large segment of the jobs in the U.S. economy in this context is found in *Estimates of Worker Traits Characteristics for 4000 Jobs*.[15] In this volume, the United States Employment Service estimated various job-related characteristics for a sample of 4000 jobs drawn from the second edition of the *Dictionary of Occupational Titles*. The nature of these estimates can be briefly summarized. Employment service personnel rated the job descriptions (not observed jobs) by levels of general and specific training required, and the aptitudes, interests, temperaments, and working conditions which characterize each worker-job relationship. The estimates of required Specific Vocational Preparation (SVP) were made on a training-time basis; the General Educational Development (GED) estimates can be converted to school-year equivalents.[16] GED and SVP requirements are defined as "the amounts of educational development and vocational preparation necessary for a worker to have acquired the knowledges and abilities essential for average performance in a given job."[17] The temperament, interest, and working-condition estimates given have no clear relationship to job evaluation, but some of the aptitude estimates are of considerable interest. The aptitudes for which relative requirements have been estimated are: 1) general intelligence; 2) verbal ability; 3) numerical ability; 4) spatial perception; 5) form perception; 6) clerical perception; 7) motor coordination; 8) finger dexterity; 9) manual dexterity; 10) eye-hand-foot coordination; and 11) color discrimination ability.

The 4000 jobs for which these estimates exist were then allocated by the author to the three-digit census occupations through the detailed titles given in the *Classified Index of Occupations*. This latter volume contains all the household responses which were placed in each detailed census group. In the absence of employment data for the 4000 jobs, it was necessary to obtain the estimates for census occupations as unweighted averages of the estimates for their component jobs. The mean number of jobs per census occupation was nineteen, although the titles of "operatives, n.e.c. [not elsewhere classified]" and "laborers, n.e.c." contained several hundred.[18]

Most of these training and aptitude characteristics reflect the requirements of job content or particular facets of it, although with an unfortunate emphasis on blue-collar skills. They should be related to the sorts of training, abilities, skills, and responsibilities for which wages are presumably the reward. On this assumption, an attempt was made to estimate the prices paid in the market for each of these characteristics. The "value" of a job in this model would thus be the sum of the market valuations of its constituent requirements. The parallel with usual job-evaluation procedures is clear, in which point-values are attached to various demands upon the worker, including skill requirements, and the point totals are translated into dollars. "Market prices" for these characteristics were estimated by a regression of training and aptitude requirements on 1960 median occupational earnings.

The estimating equation is presented in Table 2, wherein the dependent variable was the 1960 median full-time wage and salary income for males, with observations on 204 occupations. The regression was stopped at the point where insignificant variables began to crop up in the step-wise regression. Since many of the aptitude traits are highly collinear, including all the variables would lead to fluctuating weights and rather random estimates of significance.

The level of R^2 was .33, significant at the 1 per cent level. The levels of general educational development, numerical ability, and spatial perception are directly related to compensation, with ability to discriminate colors hav-

Table 2. The regression equation used to estimate provisional values of jobs.[a]

Variable	Beta weight	Regression coefficient	t-test
Intercept	—	3843.51	3.13
General education	.3570	+183.28	4.31
Numerical ability	.1692	+333.15	2.07
Spatial perception	.1685	+343.11	2.63
Color discrimination ability	−.1699	−371.01	−2.85

[a] The Bureau of Employment Security (BES) aptitude estimates have been rearranged from their original form, so that 5 represents a high level of the trait, and 1 a low level. The BES figures are vice versa.

ing a negative effect. It is somewhat surprising that specific vocational preparation time is not significant, but these levels are highly correlated $(+.7)$ with levels of GED.

For any occupation, the regression estimate is conceived to be the wage an occupation would command on the basis of these aspects of job content. The equation showed that the required level of general educational development was most significant in affecting relative occupational incomes. Only three of the aptitudes had a significant impact on income level, but the regression "explained" 33 per cent of the variance in median occupational incomes. To explore the importance of some factors not associated with job content, the following characteristics of job-holders were added to the equation: median age and the percentage of male, urban, and Negro workers for each occupation. As expected, positive contributions to the level of earnings can be attributed to age, the percentage of male and urban workers, and a negative differential for the percentage of Negroes. The result of this second step was to raise the fraction of explained earning variance from .33 to .59. We should expect much of the remaining variance to be explained by variables not considered here: returns to scarce or peculiar combinations of the thirteen factors, regional and industrial characteristics of occupations, and returns to unionism or supply restrictions of various types.

The unweighted mean earnings of all occupations in 1960 were about $5300; the standard deviation of the regression equation estimates about $450. On this basis, census occupations were placed provisionally into five levels, according to the estimated value of their training and aptitudes. Occupations with regression estimates more than three standard deviations above the mean—roughly speaking, estimated value of $6700 or more—were placed on level I. Those more than three standard deviations below (that is, estimated value less than $3900) were placed on level V. Between these two extremes, three levels were established by dividing the $2800 range into roughly equal parts. Thus, level II occupations had estimated values between $5800 and $6700. Level III spanned estimates from $4800 to $5800, and the range from $3900 to $4800 was designated level IV. It was not felt useful to establish levels more than three standard deviations from the mean—only eight of the fifty-eight level I or V occupations lay more than four standard deviations away. The allocation of census titles to the job families and job-content levels is shown in Appendix I, along with their GED and SVP requirements, and their values estimated by the regression.

It is important to recognize that, although this process introduces an empirical basis for the ranking of occupations, and especially for interfamily comparisons, the role of judgment cannot be completely eliminated. The decision that five is the maximum number of levels which the quality of the data can support provides one example. Secondly, some occupations were clearly out of line. Perhaps the clearest example was the case of title 621, "auto service and parking attendants." The GED and SVP estimates of 11.00 and 1.69 years, respectively, are highly suspect, and would lead to considerable overvaluation. Hence this occupation and several others with similar problems were demoted. A few occupations were also upgraded from external knowledge of their requirements relative to other occupations, particularly those where the skill characteristics used did not adequately reflect the demands of the job.

CONCEPTUAL AND PRACTICAL
PROBLEMS OF CLASSIFICATION

The question of the meaningfulness and value of summation across job families by job-content level has been raised earlier. Such a summation implies that there is a certain comparability among jobs at the various content levels, regardless of the technical focus or job family. Certainly such a procedure will suppress important information yielded by the job-family breakdown. Nevertheless, in terms of the over-all balance of the "demands which . . . the job makes . . . on workers" in our economy, such summation will yield an index of jobs at various levels of complexity. On the unskilled level, a job-content total reflects people of similar skills and abilities employed in fairly simple jobs. These jobs and these workers are fairly homogeneous, so that this summation poses few problems. At the higher levels of job content, however, a total across this level does not imply that the jobs or the workers are highly similar—it should in fact mean the very opposite. On this level, jobs have in common a high degree of complexity and are often quite specialized. This is the sort of information which a set of content-level totals yields without ignoring the meaningful differences among jobs in the different job families.

In the process of classification, problems arise from the broad nature of the census occupational data. Not only do the occupations contain wide ranges of technical job foci as discussed in Chapter 1, but even a fairly straightforward occupation is found at many different levels of job content. Thus, the assignment of a particular census occupation to a job-content level will often conceal wide ranges of duties, skills, and abilities. For example, "cooks" vary from the highly talented chef to the proprietor of a hot dog stand. Similar examples could be multiplied indefinitely. Nevertheless, if the number of *D.O.T.* jobs in the census occupation is large enough, classification to a particular content level should be less sensitive to missing information. More perniciously, some occupational groups are broad enough to allow debate on what the major focus is, and therefore which is the relevant job family. Such factors add to the difficulty of classification and can only be remedied by more detailed data more accurately pinpointing the job foci and levels of job content involved.

An important conceptual and practical flaw of the empirical measurement of job content lies in the changing content of occupations over time. This may happen either by changes in the relative size of various suboccupations or by changes in the jobs themselves. In the second case, there are many examples of craft occupations retaining the same name but having very different job content as time passes: the machinist classification now covers many jobs that would not have fallen under the earlier craft definition. Similarly, the development of new techniques and the expansion of knowledge have radically affected the job content of physicians and surgeons.

Table 3. Male income by family and content level, 1960.

Job family	I	II	III	IV	V	Total
Total	6797	6586	5247	4283	3917	5319
Tools—specialized	4888	5853	5446	4491	3619	4972
Tools—nonspecialized	6136	5921	5352	3606	3999	4910
Machines—specialized	—	6001	4908	4975	—	5141
Machines—nonspecialized	—	—	6203	5330	4909	5038
Inspection	—	6622	5812	4657	2803	6472
Vehicle operation	—	7374	4797	5412	3714	4804
Farm	—	3936	3777	2500	1910	2305
Sales A	6894	6253	4575	—	—	5942
Sales B	—	—	5035	5566	960	5177
Clerical	6611	5669	5309	4934	3020	5339
Personal service	—	—	3927	3470	3085	3356
Entertainment	6046	7091	5194	4583	2465	5196
Protection	—	—	5365	4420	4485	5018
Education	6298	—	—	—	—	6298
Health	6794	5972	4932	3344	—	5878
Welfare	4405	4146	—	—	—	4384
Admin. & organization	8394	7433	5986	7487	3817	6912
Research & design	8368	6040	—	—	—	8011

Characteristics of the job-content matrix. The 200-odd occupations for which census data exist were allocated to the various job families and job-content levels in accordance with the concepts, procedures, and judgments outlined above. A complete listing is shown in Appendix I, along with the code number from the 1950 *Classified Index of Occupations* which reveals the census social-economic group from which each occupation is drawn. Appendix II contains a statistical test of the present experimental classification, which conforms with theoretical expectations outlined in this chapter. The following tables display some characteristics of the various cells of the job-content matrix.

In Tables 3 and 4, estimates are shown of median full-time wage and salary income for each group by sex for 1960. There are considerable differences in the levels of income by job families, and, within the job families, income levels vary directly with the level of job content. Furthermore, there are important differences in median income between the two sexes which arise from differing importance of the various job families and of content levels within the families.

Table 4. Female income by family and content level, 1960.

Job family	I	II	III	IV	V	Total
Total	4426	4013	3397	2361	2042	3161
Tools—specialized	n.a.	3531	3279	2556	2017	2361
Tools—nonspecialized	3679	3767	3694	2011	2878	2857
Machines—specialized	—	3678	3057	2756	—	2994
Machines—nonspecialized	—	—	4473	n.a.	3038	—
Inspection	—	3885	3928	n.a.	2146	3700
Vehicle operation	—	—	2788	—	2386	—
Farm	—	—	—	—	898	—
Sales A	3943	3769	3145	—	—	3734
Sales B	—	—	2867	2336	848	2304
Clerical	4335	3144	3535	2848	2317	3548
Personal service	—	—	2305	1987	1192	1515
Entertainment	2298	4614	3257	n.a.	1995	2452
Protection	—	—	3879	3442	n.a.	—
Education	4643	—	—	—	—	4643
Health	5346	3843	3819	2279	—	3149
Welfare	4406	2605	—	—	—	3860
Admin. & organization	4703	4345	2766	4341	1397	3675
Research & design	5258	4702	—	—	—	5145

Table 5. Male schooling by family and content level, 1960.

Job family	I	II	III	IV	V	Total
Total	16.3	12.2	11.4	10.4	9.2	11.0
Tools—specialized	12.5	11.6	10.7	9.5	8.7	10.3
Tools—nonspecialized	12.0	10.9	10.1	8.7	8.8	9.7
Machines—specialized	—	11.8	9.3	8.6	—	9.5
Machines—nonspecialized	—	—	11.0	8.9	9.4	9.7
Inspection	—	11.7	12.1	9.9	8.2	11.7
Vehicle operation	—	10.7	9.6	10.2	10.6	9.8
Farm	—	11.5	9.0	8.7	8.1	8.3
Sales A	12.6	12.9	10.9	—	—	12.4
Sales B	—	—	12.3	12.3	9.1	12.0
Clerical	15.3	13.4	12.5	12.2	10.4	12.8
Personal service	—	—	9.6	9.0	9.6	9.4
Entertainment	14.4	15.6	13.2	12.1	10.2	13.3
Protection	—	—	12.2	8.9	8.5	11.0
Education	17.1	—	—	—	—	17.1
Health	17.4	15.0	13.3	10.6	—	15.4
Welfare	16.9	16.3	—	—	—	16.9
Admin. & organization	16.8	13.0	12.2	12.1	9.4	12.9
Research & design	16.2	12.9	—	—	—	15.7

Table 6. Female schooling by family and content level, 1960.

Job family	I	II	III	IV	V	Total
Total	15.9	12.8	12.2	11.1	9.2	12.1
Tools—specialized	12.7	12.0	10.9	9.5	8.9	9.4
Tools—nonspecialized	11.0	10.3	10.7	8.8	8.9	9.6
Machines—specialized	—	12.0	9.0	7.8	—	8.8
Machines—nonspecialized	—	—	11.5	n.a.	9.3	9.4
Inspection	—	11.3	11.9	10.8	8.6	11.1
Vehicle operation	—	n.a.	11.3	n.a.	n.a.	—
Farm	—	—	—	8.8	7.5	7.7
Sales A	12.4	12.6	11.5	—	—	12.3
Sales B	—	—	12.3	11.5	11.6	11.5
Clerical	14.4	12.9	12.4	12.0	11.8	12.4
Personal service	—	—	10.4	10.5	9.1	9.5
Entertainment	14.9	16.0	12.6	12.4	11.0	13.9
Protection	—	—	12.3	11.8	11.2	11.7
Education	16.5	—	—	—	—	16.5
Health	17.4	13.1	13.1	11.1	—	12.5
Welfare	15.9	13.4	—	—	—	15.1
Admin. & organization	14.2	13.1	11.9	12.5	11.1	12.7
Research and design	15.1	12.9	—	—	—	14.7

Table 7. Years of general educational development required, 1960.

Job family	I	II	III	IV	V	Total
Total	16.17	12.11	10.46	9.48	7.93	10.37
Tools—specialized	15.00	11.60	9.63	9.02	7.92	9.38
Tools—nonspecialized	11.46	11.53	10.89	8.15	6.34	9.52
Machines—specialized	—	11.66	9.39	7.96	—	9.22
Machines—nonspecialized	—	—	10.31	10.57	8.56	8.71
Inspection	—	11.81	11.85	10.64	7.00	11.74
Vehicle operation	—	10.68	9.30	7.38	9.82	9.39
Farm	—	16.00	12.00	10.67	8.15	9.81
Sales A	16.00	10.93	9.88	—	—	11.62
Sales B	—	—	10.22	9.12	7.94	9.07
Clerical	16.00	14.00	10.25	10.09	7.57	10.59
Personal service	—	—	11.27	8.73	7.69	8.60
Entertainment	15.58	17.33	13.33	7.00	6.79	13.90
Protection	—	—	10.41	9.17	5.50	9.81
Education	16.54	—	—	—	—	16.54
Health	17.61	14.03	11.74	9.92	—	12.54
Welfare	15.62	n.a.	—	—	—	15.62
Admin. & organization	17.14	12.79	11.43	11.00	n.a.	12.56
Research & design	15.29	12.68	—	—	—	14.89

Table 8. Years of specific vocational preparation required, 1960.

Job family	I	II	III	IV	V	Total
Total	5.27	3.18	1.63	1.12	.80	1.86
Tools—specialized	2.62	4.16	2.10	1.31	.64	1.80
Tools—nonspecialized	4.08	3.02	2.06	1.18	.45	1.77
Machines—specialized	—	2.84	1.38	1.01	—	1.49
Machines—nonspecialized	—	—	1.61	1.93	.98	1.04
Inspection	—	3.47	2.63	1.55	.21	3.29
Vehicle operation	—	3.36	82	.22	1.42	1.02
Farm	—	7.00	3.00	3.00	1.12	1.72
Sales A	7.00	2.35	.76	—	—	2.84
Sales B	—	—	.61	.82	.05	.77
Clerical	5.00	3.88	.66	.38	.10	.92
Personal service	—	—	2.35	.40	.63	.98
Entertainment	7.38	1.50	3.59	.38	.03	5.36
Protection	—	—	.60	.14	.02	.42
Education	5.41	—	—	—	—	5.41
Health	6.61	2.32	2.43	1.27	—	2.79
Welfare	4.18	n.a.	—	—	—	4.18
Admin. & organization	5.39	3.38	4.81	.04	n.a.	4.08
Research & design	4.23	2.68	—	—	—	3.99

Tables 5 and 6 display estimates of median years of school completed for the 1960 job structure by sex. There are again important differences between various job families and job-content levels. In most job families, women had lower median years of schooling than men, but the distribution of women among job families was so different from the male pattern that over-all female medians were higher. Women's employment, for example, is small in the blue-collar regions of the matrix which are relatively low in terms of formal education. It is possible, however, that in many cells of the matrix, the lower average schooling of women may be associated with genuine differences in the content of the "same" job held by a woman instead of a man.

The data of Tables 3–4 and 5–6 show strong relationships between the levels of income and formal education and the level of job content. To some extent this may derive from the use of income and training data as major parts of the model used for ranking. On the other hand, it is important to recognize that education and income are closely connected in theory with job content. The first is a prerequisite, the second is often a reward for the complexity of the job. Differences in education and income stem both from differences in the technical foci of the job families and the relative content levels within them.

Tables 7 and 8 show estimates of general educational development and specific vocational preparation requirements, respectively, for the job-content matrix of 1960. Significant differences arise in the levels of requirements of various families due to the varying relative importance of the levels of job content. In both cases the relationship between content level and educational or training requirements is very strong, and shows much wider range than the attainment estimates of Tables 5 and 6.

Table 9. Distribution of employment by job-content levels, urban-rural and white-Negro.

(per cent)

Level	Urban	Rural	"White" [a]	Negro
I	9.7	5.9	9.2	5.8
II	15.6	10.2	15.3	3.1
III	36.2	28.7	35.6	20.1
IV	14.4	24.3	17.3	12.6
V	24.1	30.9	22.6	58.4

[a] "White" includes all non-Negro, that is, Chinese and Japanese in addition to Caucasians, and so forth.

Job-content level distributions for 1960 are shown in Table 9 for two principal breakdowns of the American population. Sizable differences exist between the urban and rural job-content levels, with the rural distribution consistently at a lower level. Disparities among the job-content levels of white and Negro workers are even greater, with nearly three-fifths of all Negro workers falling at the lowest level of job content.

SUMMARY

Proceeding from the distinction between the two principal dimensions of job content, this chapter has developed a theoretical and empirical classification. Important relationships between the jobs and major technical foci were used in the development of job families. Within these families, principles of job evaluation were employed to develop a ranking by job-content levels, in which income was viewed as the result of market prices paid for various aspects of training and ability.

Chapter 3

CHANGING JOB CONTENT, 1940–1960

Changes in any employment structure have several facets, among which are regional, industrial, job family, and content-level shifts. Even age and sex distributions will be affected because of jobs in which these factors are important criteria for employment. In the final analysis, the determinants of the various movements may be quite different, and the data we see are the results of interaction of supply and demand. The demand for labor has almost as many dimensions as we care to measure, each individual job having subscripts which denote its location in place and time, industry, job family, and content level within the family. The fineness with which each characteristic is measured determines the level of analysis at which one must operate. At present, the crudeness and unwieldiness of the data allow only a fairly aggregate level of investigation.

Here is a brief summary of the factors which influence demand in each of the dimensions of employment for the facets of region, industry, job family, and job-content level. Changes in the regional structure of demand for labor will depend on the regional structure of demand for goods and services, and the structure of industry by region. Availability of natural resources and capital, transportation facilities, and other cooperating factors will enter into the determination of demand for labor by regions. Changes in the industrial composition of job demand are primarily dependent on the demand for products of that industry and the factors which cause it to change, and the changes in the demand for the various job families important in the industry. The demand for job families will reflect changes in the kinds of employment, and the skills, responsibilities, and training required. Changes in these facets of demand will depend not only on shifts in the structure of demand for products, but also on alterations in the way the product is produced—technology. It is essential to our understanding of technological change to be able to talk about the jobs which will be affected. For example, the railroad eliminated some jobs and created others—it is important to be able to compare the characteristics of both.

At any point in time, then, the job structure will be the result of the interaction of multidimensional supply and demand functions. This suggests a further point—just as supply and demand curves in a market model yield a solution in the form of a quantity-price pair, the wage structure is logically associated with the job structure itself. Some indications of this relationship are explored at the end of this chapter.

AGGREGATE CHANGES IN JOB CONTENT, 1940–1960

For a first view of the over-all changes in job content of the U.S. economy, the numbers of persons included the five job content levels are shown in Table 10 for 1940 to 1960.

These figures show the continued strong growth of the upper three job-content groups over the past two decades, with relative stability in the number of workers on lower levels. This pattern of growth has led to a considerable shift in the percentage shares of the job structure. The two top groups have expanded from one-sixth in 1940 to almost one quarter of the jobs in 1960. As seen in Table 11, all growth rates but level I fell in the second decade of weaker aggregate demand, and the drop was borne by the lower groups.

An important aspect of the change in job content over the two decades has been the differing behavior in male and female employment. Not only does the over-all distribution of the content level differ between the two sexes, but the rates of change have also diverged widely. Table 12 shows the percentage distribution by content level for the three census years for male and female employment.

Table 10. Employment in thousands by job-content level, and percentages of total, 1940–1960.

Level	1940	1950	1960
Total	44567	55485	61456
I	2703	3763	5333
II	4262	6405	8708
III	12718	18017	21002
IV	10794	11514	10461
V	14091	15786	15951
Percentages	100.0	100.0	100.0
I	6.1	6.8	8.7
II	9.6	11.5	14.2
III	28.5	32.5	34.2
IV	24.2	20.8	17.0
V	31.6	28.4	25.9

The two patterns differ markedly in each year as well as in their movements over time. The national advance in the percentage of level I workers comes entirely from shifts in male employment, while levels II and III have experienced their sharpest growth among women, largely in "clerical" areas. Declines in the percentage share of workers on lower levels have largely stemmed from changes in the male distribution.

The major portion of the total growth of employment in the past two decades has come from increases among female workers. Table 13 displays the rates of growth for the two periods. Male employment grew at rates substantially below those for female employment in both decades, and experienced a very pronounced decline in growth rate in the 1950's. Only the highest job-content level maintained its growth rate among males. Female workers, on the other hand, continued to show a strong increase.

Table 11. Aggregate demand and job-content levels, 1940–1950, 1950–1960.
(changes in per cent)

Level	1940–1950	1950–1960
I	39.2	41.7
II	50.6	35.9
III	41.7	16.5
IV	12.5	−9.1
V	12.0	1.0
GNP (1954 dollars)	54.6	38.3

Table 12. Job-content levels by sex, 1940, 1950, and 1960.
(percentage distribution)

Level	1940	1950	1960
Male	100.0	100.0	100.0
I	4.8	6.1	8.4
II	11 8	14.6	18.8
III	27.8	30.9	31.8
IV	27.0	22.6	17.5
V	28.6	25.8	23.5
Female	100.0	100.0	100.0
I	9.9	8.5	9.2
II	2.7	4.1	4.6
III	30.7	36.5	39.0
IV	15.6	16.1	15.9
V	41.1	34.8	31.3

Women found many opportunities during the fifties at the higher- and medium-content level—in inspection, sales, clerical, and welfare areas, with extraordinary growth in the administrative and research job families. During the twenty-year period, total employment rose about 17 million—women accounting for roughly 9 million of these jobs. Approximately 4.4 million were on job-content level III, and 3.5 million of these jobs were clerical.

The effect of the rapid growth of female employment on its share at the

Table 13. Growth rates of employment by sex, 1940–1950, 1950–1960.
(per cent per decade)

Level	1940–1950	1950–1960
Male	18.1	4.7
I	38.6	44.5
II	45.0	35.4
III	32.9	8.0
IV	−1.3	−18.7
V	7.3	−5.3
Female	40.5	29.1
I	22.9	36.8
II	120.5	40.9
III	71.3	34.7
IV	48.4	24.4
V	22.1	12.8

Table 14. Male percentage by job-content levels, 1940, 1950, and 1960.

Level	1940	1950	1960
Total	75.3	71.9	67.5
I	59.4	64.2	65.5
II	93.0	89.7	89.4
III	73.5	67.9	62.9
IV	84.0	77.8	69.6
V	68.0	65.1	61.0

various job-content levels is shown in Table 14. The patterns of growth of the two sexes have differed in considerable degree, and the result has been a great increase in the female share of the III and IV content levels, with the male share only increasing on level I. Women's share of the whole has advanced from one-quarter in 1940 to one-third in 1960.

REGIONAL PATTERNS OF CHANGE

The pattern of upward movement observed for the nation as a whole has also been prevalent on a regional basis, and differentials between regions have been narrowing. Table 15 presents data on employment by job-content levels for the broad regional breakdown of the census.

Table 16 shows the percentage breakdown of the four regions by content levels, revealing that the distributions of the various regions have moved toward greater similarity in the years since 1940. This trend results in part from the elimination of jobs which formerly predominated in a region as well as from the continuing diffusion of industrial activity throughout the nation. Thus, a great deal of the move toward the national percentage in lower job-content groups in the south comes from a large drop in the number of farm owners and tenants. While this group was suffering a 51 per cent nationwide decline in the twenty-year period, the decline in the south was 64 per cent—in a category that included nearly one fifth of southern employment in 1940. But a large part of the growth comes from the introduction of new jobs, not just the elimination of old ones. The number of tool and die makers in the United States doubled from 1940 to 1960—in the south the number quintupled. The same is true for many industrial jobs and skilled crafts.

For the entire twenty-year period, the west has held a high job-content level relative to the rest of the country, and seems to have gained ground slightly over this time. As well as rapid growth in the "industrial" sectors of the job-content matrix, clerical, administrative, educational, and health families also grew very quickly. This sort of shift may reflect the change in the state of economic development in the region. From a sparsely populated area

Table 15. Employment by job-content levels by major region, 1940, 1950, and 1960. (thousands)

Level	1940	1950	1960
Northeast[a]	12671	15281	16158
I	851	1128	1477
II	1432	1978	2486
III	4212	5418	5719
IV	1999	2313	2203
V	4177	4448	4273
Northcentral[b]	13632	16867	17994
I	844	1114	1497
II	1440	1990	2589
III	3983	5372	5960
IV	3380	3736	3382
V	3985	4655	4566
South[c]	13575	16251	17751
I	670	968	1400
II	884	1450	2166
III	3007	4733	5859
IV	4056	4120	3236
V	4958	4980	5090
West[d]	4686	6980	9548
I	329	551	937
II	500	838	1480
III	1541	2533	3468
IV	1098	1354	1494
V	1218	1704	2169

[a] Maine, New Hampshire, Vermont, Massachusetts, New York, Connecticut, Rhode Island, New Jersey, Pennsylvania.

[b] Ohio, Indiana, Illinois, Michigan, Wisconsin, Minnesota, Iowa, Missouri, North Dakota, South Dakota, Nebraska, Kansas.

[c] Delaware, Maryland, District of Columbia, Virginia, West Virginia, North Carolina, South Carolina, Georgia, Florida, Kentucky, Tennessee, Alabama, Mississippi, Arkansas, Louisiana, Oklahoma, Texas.

[d] Montana, Wyoming, Idaho, Colorado, New Mexico, Arizona, Nevada, Utah, California, Oregon, Washington, Alaska, Hawaii.

Table 16. Regional distribution by job-content level, 1940, 1950, and 1960.

(per cent)

Level	1940	1950	1960
Northeast[a]	100.0	100.0	100.0
I	6.7	7.4	9.1
II	11.3	12.9	15.4
III	33.2	35.5	35.4
IV	15.8	15.1	13.6
V	33.0	29.1	26.5
Northcentral[a]	100.0	100.0	100.0
I	6.2	6.6	8.3
II	10.6	11.8	14.4
III	29.2	31.8	33.1
IV	24.8	22.1	18.8
V	29.2	27.7	25.4
South[a]	100.0	100.0	100.0
I	4.9	6.0	7.9
II	6.5	8.9	12.2
III	22.2	29.1	33.0
IV	29.9	25.4	18.2
V	36.5	30.6	28.7
West[a]	100.0	100.0	100.0
I	7.0	7.9	9.8
II	10.7	12.0	15.5
III	32.9	36.3	36.3
IV	23.4	19.4	15.6
V	26.0	24.4	22.8

[a] Regions include the same classifications found in notes to Table 15.

in 1940, the whole territory (some sections in particular) grew very rapidly. Such growth demands filling in a large number of gaps in the white-collar part of the job structure. The reason for the west's historical tendency for a higher proportion of jobs concentrated at the upper job-content levels is not within the scope of this study. The need for independent craftsmen in a frontier area, the relative absence of mass-production industry in the early part of the period, and the growth of white-collar jobs all may be factors. The important point is that this method of summarizing the data has suggested a problem not otherwise immediately evident. Associated with this weighting toward higher levels of job content has been a high level of educational achievement. In 1960, persons twenty-five years of age and older had median schooling of 12.0 years in the west, compared with 10.6 for the country as a whole. Not only is the level of education important in the performance of a given job, but it greatly affects the adaptability of the labor force. "Education, although not the sole means, is the best means by which the individual and society can adjust to technological change." [1]

The northeast, in addition to its loss in the share of all jobs, has suffered deterioration as a region of relatively high job content. In the last two decades, jobs in the top three content levels have grown more rapidly in every other section of the country. The changing industrial composition of the northeast has certainly been responsible for part of this change.

Within the framework of job content, differences in the composition and change of jobs among regions are easily seen. Differences will depend on underlying characteristics of industry and population, which could be studied in greater detail. The job-content model yields information relevant to the study of regional growth and development in the United States, and could be applied to problems of national economic development. Frederick H. Harbison and Charles A. Myers have found a strong correlation between a composite index of educational attainment and the level of per capita income. [2] Each of the job groups has an associated set of education and training requirements, which could be analyzed to predict the effects of technological change and economic growth. The use of the framework of job families and content levels would yield more specific information with respect to direction and length of training.

BEHAVIOR OF VARIOUS JOB FAMILIES

Employment in each of the job families for the five levels of job content of the three censuses is shown in Table 17. Differences in the behavior of the job families and content levels are apparent throughout this table. As examples, the differing movements of the specialized and nonspecialized divisions of the tool and machine families can first be cited. Both grew in the 1940's and showed a direct relationship between the level of job content and the rate of employment increase. In the 1950's, the latter relation held true, but employment in specialized jobs suffered losses—whether the jobs focused on tools or on machines and equipment.

Jobs in the inspection family displayed strong growth in both decades, especially at the higher content levels. Many of the jobs in this group—tech-

Table 17. Employment by job family and job-content level, 1940, 1950, and 1960. (thousands)[a]

Level	Tools		Machine and equipment		Inspection	Vehicle operation	Farm	Sales A	Sales B
	specialized	nonspecialized	specialized	nonspecialized					
Total	1837	6304	981	4819	743	2127	8234	758	2564
	2539	8757	1229	6675	1143	2657	6706	1017	3482
	2370	9256	960	7386	1731	3097	3950	1266	4070
I	13	8	0	0	0	0	0	70	0
	25	10	0	0	0	0	0	142	0
	44	12	0	0	0	0	0	234	0
II	248	1172	99	0	585	153	37	441	0
	299	1918	144	0	919	180	35	562	0
	280	2310	172	0	1450	162	24	734	0
III	600	2052	160	313	121	1586	24	248	36
	875	3307	354	347	179	2045	17	313	57
	900	3548	404	423	239	2432	25	298	75
IV	512	426	721	154	14	107	5107	0	2422
	612	574	731	208	17	109	4280	0	3307
	535	705	384	172	20	85	2486	0	3750
V	465	2645	0	4352	22	282	3066	0	105
	728	2948	0	6120	29	322	2374	0	118
	611	2682	0	6790	22	419	1415	0	245

[a] In each triplet of numbers, the top figure refers to 1940. One reads down to 1950 and 1960 estimates.

	Clerical	Personal services	Entertainment	Protection	Admin. & org.	Research & design	Education	Health	Welfare	Total
Total	4434	4436	288	462	3819	424	1116	981	241	44567
	6995	4386	386	610	5039	860	1290	1421	300	55485
	9496	5415	436	722	5607	1376	1926	2000	390	61456
I	257	0	181	0	236	344	1116	272	206	2703
	432	0	231	0	322	738	1290	313	259	3762
	555	0	294	0	411	1163	1926	361	334	5333
II	39	0	12	0	1263	80	0	99	35	4262
	45	0	16	0	1914	122	0	211	41	6405
	79	0	28	0	2907	213	0	293	56	8708
III	3886	772	30	241	2226	0	0	423	0	12718
	6022	923	43	347	2711	0	0	479	0	18017
	8096	1188	34	446	2204	0	0	690	0	21002
IV	184	725	5	205	25	0	0	187	0	10794
	434	537	15	244	27	0	0	418	0	11514
	703	671	11	250	33	0	0	656	0	10461
V	68	2940	60	16	69	0	0	0	0	14091
	63	2926	82	12	66	0	0	0	0	15786
	63	3556	70	25	53	0	0	0	0	15951

nicians, manufacturing inspectors, and foremen—belong in a class mentioned in Chapter 2. It was there proposed that a distinction could usefully be made between jobs which involve the direction of machines and equipment and those which are simply adjunct to their operation. For lack of appropriate data this could not be done, but the increases in inspection jobs at level II may reflect to considerable extent the growth of jobs in the machine-direction category.

Many writers have commented on the increasing bureaucratization of the economy, and at least one has constructed part of a theory of inflation from it.[3] These tendencies are clearly reflected in Table 17, but in even finer detail. The growth in content level II (administrative and organizational family) remained steady in the second decade, growing at roughly five times the rate of the whole economy. On the other hand, level III jobs in this family, among which "managers, officials, and proprietors, n.e.c. [not elsewhere classified], self-employed" predominate, suffered an actual decline of almost 20 per cent. In essence, a sharp contrast is here presented between the growth of salaried and self-employed management personnel. Unfortunately, the broad spectrum of jobs included at the two administrative levels makes it impossible to answer more specific related questions. The increase in salaried personnel might represent increasing bureaucracy, or it may in part reflect the tax advantages which accrue to small business from adopting this form of organization.

Clerical and sales job families grew more rapidly than the national totals, and, in general, growth within each family was correlated with the level of job content. In addition, growth was more rapid in sales jobs which involve considerable knowledge of the product or service as part of job content.

It is generally known that service employment is rapidly increasing, but in Table 17 jobs of this type are split into several classes—personal services, health, protection, and so on—each of which behaves somewhat differently. The table also shows higher-level services in the fields of education, entertainment, and welfare. The behavior of employment among the various types of service workers is especially interesting in view of the changes in the aggregate demand situation from the forties to the fifties. In the family of personal service workers, level III jobs grew fairly rapidly in both decades, although more rapidly in the decade of weaker demand buoyancy. The level IV and level V personal service occupations decreased by 27.5 per cent in the 1940's. However, the weaker aggregate demand situation of the 1950's saw an increase of 20.8 per cent in this group, accompanied by a rate of income increase of 37 per cent—far below the national median of 72 per cent. Growth of these lower-level personal service occupations, to many of which workers turn when better, higher-paying jobs are not available, was a direct result of the decline in the rate of economic growth.

Protection workers show rapid growth at level III, and slower growth among the lower-skilled workers. The health family figures reflect a change in the technological situation of the family and the industry with which it roughly coincides, with the ancillary or "paramedical" workers growing very swiftly over the past twenty years.[4]

Comparison with the social-economic groups. It is instructive to compare the information yielded by the scheme of job structure with that of the present census data. Employment by social-economic groups for 1940, 1950, and 1960 is shown in Table 18.

Although a certain amount of job content and skill difference underlies the social-economic grouping, it is not sufficiently apparent in the data. This criticism is especially appropriate in regard to differences within the social-economic groups. There are broad ranges of job content in most of the groups (for example, sales workers range from stockbrokers to peddlers, and professional workers range from professors to faith healers).

The job-content classification also displays considerably more information about the main focus of jobs in the economy. The prime example is in the area of services, where the type of service performed is certainly important. In addition, as we have seen, the behavior of various service groups has been highly disparate. Any attempt to discuss them as a whole will ignore interesting and significant information. Further examples of important trends revealed by the content classification (but concealed in Table 18) can be given: the growth of inspection jobs, the differing movements of two basic types of administrative personnel, and the change in the job-content balance

Table 18. Employment in census social-economic groups, 1940 to 1960.
(thousands)

Census group	1940	1950	1960
Professional, technical, etc.	3580	4921	7232
Managers, officials, proprietors	8782	9348	7915
Clerical and kindred workers	4382	6954	9307
Sales and kindred workers	3081	3907	4639
Craftsmen, foremen, etc.	5171	7821	8741
Operatives and kindred workers	8080	11180	11898
Service workers	5292	5708	7171
Laborers and kindred workers	6285	5853	4552

of the health family. Our information about changes in the jobs people perform has clearly been increased.

A side effect of changing job content—wage interdependence. If the theory underlying the job-content model is correct, then another effect must be considered—the linkage between the various jobs in the same cell of the matrix. If the jobs found in a single cell have similar skill, ability, and training characteristics, then wage changes should be similar to the same degree throughout the box. A manageable example might be found in job-content level III of the clerical family for which female employment and income data are shown in Table 19.

There is an insignificant correlation between the rate of change of income and that of employment.[5] But more important, only one job stands clearly out of line with the rest in terms of wage changes: bank tellers, who had the highest rate of growth, yet the lowest income rise. This was presumably related to the very slow growth of income in the banking industry as a whole, coupled with a shift from male to female tellers. Income in the other occupations moved quite closely together despite disparities in their rates of employment change. Such a result is in conformity with theoretical expectation, as the concept of job family is related to that of job clusters on the plant level.

Table 19. Employment and income changes (level III female clerical jobs), 1950 to 1960.

(per cent)

Occupation	Change	
	Female full-time wage and salary income (median)	*Female employment*
Telephone operators	61	−1
Telegraph operators	69	−40
Stenographers	61	40
Office machine operators	61	94
Bookkeepers	57	37
Ticket agents	62	101
Bank tellers	50	218
Agents, n.e.c.[a]	70	43
Clerical workers, n.e.c.[a]	60	21

[a] Not elsewhere classified.

That the rates of change of employment in the particular job and in the surrounding job group are very likely cumulative factors influencing changes in wages is suggested by Table 20. The fourteen occupations in the two tool job families, on content level II, are shown with their male income and employment changes from 1950 to 1960. The occupations have been placed in four classes on the basis of employment changes in both job and group. In class 1 are the jobs where both employment changes were positive; in class 4, both negative. On the moderate content level, the specialized branches of both job families lost employment during the period.

Spot inspection tells us that the levels of income changes are different in the four classes. The median increase of income in class 1, where group and job employment both increased, was 74 per cent. In class 4, where employment in the job and in the surrounding group declined, the median

Table 20. Percentage increases in median male full-time wage and salary income and employment in the tool job families (level II), classed by employment behavior of job and job group, 1950–1960.

Class and job	Income	Employment
Class 1 (where employment increased in both job and group)		
Toolmakers and diemakers	74	19
Patternmakers, except paper	80	8
Millwrights	78	11
Job setters	71	63
Tinsmiths	70	10
Mechanics, n.e.c.[a]	70	34
Class 2 (where employment increased in the group but fell in the particular job)		
Cabinetmakers	64	−10
Machinists	71	−3
Class 3 (where employment increased in the particular job but fell for the whole group)		
Compositors and typesetters	58	2
Class 4 (where employment in both job and group fell)		
Photoengravers	49	−13
Loom fixers	42	−21
Jewelers	54	−20
Piano tuners	n.a.[b]	−22
Electrotypers	43	−24

[a] Not elsewhere classified.

[b] Not available due to small size of income sample.

increase of income was 47 per cent. In classes 2 and 3, where the two effects went in opposite directions, the median wage increase was 67 and 58 per cent respectively. More data would be needed to test the hypothesis suggested by the latter figures—that the group movement exerts larger influence than that of the particular job.

The existence of such a pattern should be noted for two reasons: 1) the analysis of side effects, and 2) the job-content model itself. Prediction and analysis of wage pressures and patterns likely to be associated with the changing structure of employment depend on knowledge of the mechanisms involved. A theory of wage determination which puts emphasis on "clusters" of jobs and on key jobs, while not coterminous with the procedures used in this study, is closely allied with the families and content levels employed here. The job-content approach may therefore prove useful in the analysis of changes in wage structure arising from changing patterns of industrial demand and changing technology.

Also, if this is a good approximation to the theory, and if pay scales do tend to move similarly within the boxes constructed, we have a fairly good test of the success of the system and the procedures involved in the allocation of occupations to parts of the matrix. Since the jobs in any cell of the matrix are supposed to be more like each other than like outside jobs in the area of skill, responsibility, and work methods, the wage rates should move together. The fact that they do can be seen in Table 19 and in the data of Table 20, if rearranged by job-family breaks. But the interaction effects, shown in Table 20, from the change of employment in the job and in the surrounding group, appear extremely important. Further research on these points, especially with regard to job-family impact on wage movements in the various cells of the job-content matrix, is presented in Appendix II.

Other possible side effects. Still other side effects could be examined in the same fashion, assuming the existence of appropriate data. For example, perhaps some part of the national median income increase could be attributed to changes in the regional distribution of various jobs. This category would include changes in the national median because of alterations in the balance of employment between high- and low-wage regions, as well as wage increases stemming from the spatial separation of supply and demand. Undoubtedly other factors have been ignored in my necessarily brief treatment: how much of the 85 per cent increase of median income of professional workers, n.e.c., has arisen from changes in the jobs included in this category? This study cannot encompass all such problems, but the questions could still be discussed in the framework of job content.

The effects of content change on educational and training requirements are a subject of great concern. The data are elusive, however, and either do not give the desired measurement or rest upon weak methodology. To discuss the educational impact of changes in job content, the following items are needed: formal educational attainment, apprenticeship training, vocational and night school programs, on-the-job training, training in the armed forces—and a scheme for weighting the contributions of each. Some of these data exist on a census basis, but most do not. We shall return to some specific examples of training requirements in Chapter 5.

There is, however, incorporated in the breakdown of job content one rough indicator of the type of training required for various blue-collar jobs. The tool and machine and equipment job families were subdivided into specialized and nonspecialized groups. These figures should give an indication of the movements of jobs requiring specialized as opposed to more general skills, abilities, and training. The data for these groups show that specialized occupations declined in the fifties after considerable growth in the preceding decade, while nonspecialized jobs suffered less from the altered demand situation. In both groups, there was a rise in the relative weight of upper-level jobs in terms of job content. This, in rough fashion, indicates a general movement toward greater training and skill requirements and also toward more general, less specialized, content in these jobs.

SUMMARY

Over the past twenty years, the share of the top three job-content groups has risen in the United States. Among men, the sharpest increase has been in levels I and II; among women, level II and III jobs have grown most rapidly. There has been a continued tendency toward homogeneity in the various regions of the country, in terms of the over-all balance of job content.

The various job families and content levels within them have grown at widely differing rates. At one extreme, the growth of professional services (such as health, education, and welfare) and administrative and inspection jobs was highlighted. On the other hand, the decline of the buoyancy of aggregate demand led to sharp employment increases in personal service jobs at the lower-content level in the decade of the 1950's. These jobs suffered considerable deterioration in their relative income position as a result.

As a prime example of the side effects of changes in the employment structure, the interdependence of income changes within the groups of the job-content matrix was noted. Such a finding is of importance both for purposes of analysis and prediction and for the support it gives to the concept of job content.

The conceptual basis of job content in the clusters and families of individual firms, focused around a characteristic tool or function, was developed in Chapter 2. At the same time it was recognized that the present form of the census data required a more deductive approach. Thus the empirical classification attempted in this chapter must be regarded as an experiment. Fuller and more detailed data on jobs would allow a more informative display of job families and content levels. It is one purpose of this study to suggest a new scheme about which improved forms of data collection could be centered.

Chapter 4

PROJECTIONS TO 1970

Existing employment projections are in the form of either estimates of total employment or of particular occupations and social-economic groups. Neither of these basic types is directly applicable to the projection of job content. Furthermore, projections on a detailed level do not exist for all census occupations, so that an estimating procedure must be developed. Projections are required for several reasons—to enlighten the speculation about the effects of automation, to assist in vocational guidance and training, and to aid in the planning of educational systems. In addition, the development of a system of projections based on job content, because of its relationship to wage structure, may assist us in predicting developments in that area.

THE NATIONAL PLANNING ASSOCIATION (NPA) PROJECTIONS

The National Planning Association has developed a detailed set of output and employment projections to the years 1976 and 2000, which have been conveniently summarized and discussed in a report of the Outdoor Recreation Resources Review Commission.[1] The relative completeness of the data makes it possible to derive estimates of job content. Adjustments will be made to yield information for the next census date of 1970, to maintain our content data on a decennial basis.

The principal NPA data which relate to this study are the projections of industrial employment and its regional distribution. Gross product originating in the various major industries was projected to 1976 and 2000 on the basis of full employment (96 per cent of the labor force). Changes in productivity, measured by gross product originating per man-hour, were taken into account in determining the estimates of employment by the twelve major industry groups. In this study, it will be assumed that the annual employment growth rate for each industry predicted by the NPA for 1957–1976 will also be the average for the period from 1960–1970. On this basis, Table 21 displays the average annual growth rates and the 1970 employment level relative to a 1960 level of 100 for twelve broad industries.

The National Planning Association has also prepared estimates of the distribution of employment in the various industries among the major regions of the United States. The data, shown in Table 22, will be useful in projecting the relative levels of job content in the different parts of the country in 1970.

PROCEDURES FOR ESTIMATION OF JOB CONTENT

Job-content matrices for fifteen major industries are shown in Appendix IV for 1950 and 1960. Estimates will be developed in this form for 1970, based not only on changes in the total employment of each industry but

Table 21. Projected growth rates of employment, 1960–1970.

Industry[a]	Annual rate	Index, 1960 = 100
Agriculture	−1.7	84.2
Mining	−0.1	99.0
Construction	2.9	133.1
Manufacturing—durables	1.4	114.9
Manufacturing—nondurables	0.5	105.1
Transportation	−0.1	99.0
Communications	1.5	116.1
Utilities	1.9	120.7
Trade	2.5	128.0
Finance	1.7	118.4
Services	3.1	135.7
Public administration	1.9	120.7

Source: Outdoor Recreation Resources Review Commission, *Study Report* 23, p. 267.
[a] Census classification.

also on changes in the relative importance of various jobs within each industry. In order to take account of probable changes in the job-content matrix of each industry, while remaining at the NPA-projected total, a plausible assumption was made about changes in relative input coefficients for the various groups of jobs. It was assumed that the number of percentage-point changes in any job group's share of an industry's employment from 1950 to 1960 would be repeated in the coming decade.

An example will make this procedure clearer. Suppose that clerical workers at the highest content level had represented 10 per cent of the employ-

Table 22. Regional distribution of employment by major industry, 1957–1976.

(per cent)

Industry[a]	Employment					
	Northeast			Northcentral		
	1957	1970	1976	1957	1970	1976
Agriculture	8.1	7.7	7.5	35.6	35.9	36.0
Mining	13.2	10.3	8.9	17.2	16.3	15.9
Construction	24.9	25.4	25.7	28.9	27.1	26.3
Manufacturing	34.3	32.7	31.9	34.2	32.8	32.2
Transportation	28.7	27.3	26.7	29.6	28.0	27.5
Trade	27.5	26.7	26.3	29.9	28.6	28.0
Finance	36.2	33.7	32.5	27.0	26.1	25.7
Services	31.5	31.0	30.8	27.8	26.6	26.0
Government	23.9	24.4	24.6	25.7	25.1	24.8
	South			*West*		
Industry	1957	1970	1976	1957	1970	1976
Agriculture	43.9	42.5	41.9	12.4	13.9	14.6
Mining	52.8	55.8	57.2	16.8	17.6	18.0
Construction	30.0	30.1	30.1	16.2	17.4	17.9
Manufacturing	20.7	21.8	22.3	10.8	12.7	13.6
Transportation	26.4	27.7	28.2	15.3	16.5	17.1
Trade	27.8	28.4	28.7	14.8	16.3	17.0
Finance	22.7	24.9	25.9	14.1	15.3	15.9
Services	24.9	25.8	26.2	15.8	16.6	17.0
Government	32.0	27.4	25.4	18.4	23.1	25.2

Source: National Planning Association, *Study Report* 23, pp. 354–415. For a listing of the states in each of the four regions, see Table 15, Chap. 3.

[a] Census classification.

Table 23. United States: job-content level.
(per cent)

Level	1940	1950	1960	1970
I	6.1	6.8	8.7	9.4
II	9.6	11.5	14.2	16.1
III	28.5	32.5	34.2	34.7
IV	24.5	20.8	17.0	15.8
V	31.6	28.4	25.9	24.0

ment of an industry in 1950, and had grown to 12 per cent in 1960. Thus the estimate of their share in 1970 would be 14 per cent. In the absence of better information more firmly grounded in knowledge of technology and market changes, this procedure has two advantages. In the first place, it will yield estimates of change reasonable in the light of past experience. Further, it has the advantage of operational simplicity: the estimates are easy to obtain, and the totals for the various industries can be used as a control. Other assumptions naturally could be made; these estimates are primarily intended to illustrate the use of projections based on job families and content levels.

The numbers generated by this method are found in Tables 25 and 26 (Table 25 on an industry basis, and Table 26 on a job-family basis). The projected national content-level percentages are displayed in Table 23 along with the figures for 1940, 1950, and 1960. At this highly aggregated level, the method of estimation yields results generally in line with historical experience. The upper three job-content levels continue to gain, with relative losses in the lower two brackets. As shown in Table 24, the rates of growth for the five levels are generally within the ranges established by past experience, although closer to those of the 1940's.

Table 24. Historical and projected rates of growth.
(per cent per decade)

Level	1940–1950	1950–1960	1960–1970
Total	24.5	10.8	19.2
I	39.2	41.7	29.5
II	50.6	35.9	35.7
III	41.7	16.5	20.9
IV	12.5	−9.1	10.3
V	12.0	10.8	10.3

Table 25. Employment in industry by job-content levels, 1970.
(thousands)

Industry[a]	I	II	III	IV	V	Total
Total	6906	11821	25397	11502	17634	73260
Agriculture	28	72	231	2140	1204	3675
Mining	57	143	234	204	3	641
Construction	192	734	3053	152	908	5039
Manufacturing—durables	905	2937	2993	649	3585	11069
Manufacturing— nondurables	329	1637	1836	550	3569	7921
Transportation	35	401	1798	114	332	2680
Communications	79	203	616	38	10	946
Utilities	60	289	501	53	170	1073
Trade	534	1854	4498	4896	3144	14926
Finance	75	1229	1653	142	54	3153
Services	4214	1967	5426	2238	4437	18282
Government	398	355	2558	364	180	3855

[a] Census classification.

Table 26. Employment by job families and job-content levels, 1970.

Job family	I	II	III	IV	V	Total
Tools—specialized	76	250	1004	445	506	2281
Tools—nonspecialized	14	2878	4024	838	2466	10220
Machines—specialized	—	221	493	229	—	943
Machines—nonspecialized	—	—	501	109	7160	7770
Inspection	—	2134	337	20	18	2509
Vehicle operation	—	158	2999	69	618	3844
Farm	—	22	32	1954	1118	3126
Sales A	394	851	384	—	—	1629
Sales B	—	—	117	4747	394	5258
Clerical	793	126	10530	1113	64	12626
Personal services	—	—	1712	732	5107	7551
Entertainment	346	38	39	8	85	516
Protection	—	—	595	255	46	796
Education	2386	—	—	—	—	2386
Health	369	393	875	992	—	2629
Welfare	355	65	—	—	—	420
Administrative & org.	465	4347	1754	30	15	6611
Research & design	1709	336	—	—	—	2045

Table 27. Estimates of national and regional distributions by job-content level projected for 1970.

(per cent)

Area	I	II	III	IV	V
United States	9.4	16.1	34.7	15.8	24.0
Northeast	10.0	17.1	34.9	13.5	24.5
Northcentral	9.0	16.3	33.6	16.1	25.0
South	9.1	15.3	34.5	17.7	23.4
West	9.7	15.5	36.2	15.8	22.8

The shares of major industries by regions in 1976 as projected by the NPA are shown in Table 22. To create regional job-content estimates for 1970, it was assumed that projected share of employment changes would occur linearly over the nineteen-year period from 1957 to 1976. Thus the first thirteen years to 1970 would include thirteen nineteenths of the change to 1976. In this fashion, the 1970 projected distribution shown in the middle column of Table 22 was derived. When these figures were applied to the industry estimates of Table 24, the regional job-content distributions shown in Table 27 were reached. The detailed estimates by region, industry, and job-content level are displayed in Table 38 of Appendix III.

In the estimates shown in Table 27, continuation of historical trends is clearly projected. The northeastern and northcentral regions will maintain their positions as slightly higher and slightly lower respectively than the rest of the nation in over-all job-content distribution. The west will remain on a higher level than the country as a whole, but its relative advantage will probably be sharply reduced. Table 27 projects a continued forward surge by the south, to such a point that it may almost achieve a parity with the rest of the nation. In short, our projections portray the continued homogenization of job content in the United States by regions, as well as the continued rise in the over-all levels of job content.

The figures in Table 26 show the projected 1970 employment in the eighteen job families and their five job-content levels. Table 39 of Appendix III compares the projected rates of growth for the coming decade with those of the past two decades. For each of the 90 cells of the job-content matrix, we find a comparison of the projected growth and the "natural limits" on growth depending on the buoyancy of aggregate demand, suggested by the experience of the previous two decades. If in any part of the matrix, the natural capacity to change is regarded in relative (percentage) terms, then these figures must be assessed for an indication of the nature and location of problems which will confront our economy. We can compare the shifts projected with the movements experienced in the past and see where (if at all) binds are likely to develop.

The general conclusions from Table 39 can be briefly summarized. Rates of growth in the blue-collar sectors of the job structure will generally continue to be low or negative, with the specialized tool and machine families suffering more heavily. Continued strong growth is projected for the inspection, clerical, health, and research job families. These families are expected to grow at about the same rates as they did from 1950 to 1960. Strong growth is also projected for sales, vehicle operation, and personal service families, and at rates higher than those of the preceding decade. The rates of decline for farm jobs are on the whole expected to be halved. Relatively slow growth, but at an increased rate, is predicted for the entertainment and administrative job families. Welfare, education, and protection families should show slower growth rates. Rates of growth will continue to be strongly correlated with level of job content both on an aggregate basis and within the various job families. In Chapter 5 some probable economic consequences of such a pattern of growth will be investigated.

A critique of the projections of job content. It has been necessary to devise a means of estimating 1970 job content from the industrial employment projections of the National Planning Association. For several conceptual and practical reasons, these estimates are only speculative. They must therefore be used with great caution and be viewed primarily as examples of the predictive value of the conception of job structure developed above.

In the first place, percentage-point changes from 1950 to 1960 in job content shares have simply been extrapolated for another decade. This may be criticized on two grounds. Although such estimates will be consistent with the experience of the 1950's, we cannot compare these changes with those from 1940 to 1950. Computational difficulties prevent the collection of job-content data by industry for the earlier year. Furthermore, the economic logic is not perfect, as we have coupled the industry job-content changes of a decade of relatively weak growth with the NPA projections of fairly strong growth to 1976. This procedure should almost inevitably lead to estimated rates of growth which lie between the extremes of the two previous decades. In view of the lack of more adequate methods of projection, these are necessary evils which must be kept in mind while using the data.

In the creation of regional estimates, it was assumed that nationally projected totals of employment by industry could be distributed at all levels

Table 28. Distribution of job-content level in the personal service family by region, 1960.

(per cent)

Area	III	IV	V
Northeast	22.1	12.3	65.6
Northcentral	24.2	8.2	67.6
South	19.4	8.3	72.3
West	23.5	11.4	65.1

of job content among regions by the estimates of Table 22. This procedure implicitly assumes that broad industries are homogeneous with respect to job content across regions. This assumption can be presumed to be incorrect. Data on an industrial-regional basis cannot be conveniently developed to test this point, but the various job families do show striking differences among regions. For example, consider the data in Table 28, which show how much more heavily employment in the south in the personal service family is weighted toward level V, and the sizable regional differences. Since the NPA projections are on an industry basis, it is important to assess accurately the bias from this source. Nevertheless, it is clear that the assumption of interregional homogeneity applied to data such as those in Table 28 will produce a bias toward projection of continued equalization of regions as shown in Table 27. This may account for much of the rapid rise of the south and relative decline in the west projected above.

A third criticism stems from the industrial nature of the projections at hand. A projected growth rate of 3.1 per cent per year for the service industry must be applied to both college professors and bootblacks, since the vast majority of both occupations lies in this industry. In conjunction with the assumption discussed above, this should also tend to produce an unjustified projection of interregional homogenization.

Finally, we are confronted with a considerable gap between the total employment estimate of 73.3 million for 1970 shown by Table 25 and the NPA's own 1970 figure of 80.9 million. This discrepancy comes from two main sources. First, annual rates of growth are supposed by the NPA to be higher in the earlier part of the 1957–1976 period, whereas we have assumed constancy over the nineteen-year interval. In addition, this study has projected from 1960 census data as a benchmark, and employment in 1960 was almost 2 million below the National Planning Association's estimates for that year.

Table 29. Occupations and industries not reported in the censuses of 1950 and 1960.

Information missing	Number (000)		Percentage of total employment	
	1950	1960	1950	1960
Total	953	3368	1.71	5.21
Occupation not reported	173	756	.31	1.17
Industry not reported	236	186	.42	.29
Neither reported	544	2426	.97	3.75

The second main source of divergence lies in the fact that we have used census data on employment by occupation and industry, while the NPA figures are based on total employment. A large number of people do not report an occupation, an industry (or both) to the census. This category grew very rapidly from 1950 to 1960, primarily because of the change in the procedures for collecting data. The small sample data of 1950 were presumably collected more scrupulously than the larger sample of 1960. Table 29 shows the relevant figures. While total employment was growing by about 15 per cent, failure to report occupation or industry rose by 250 per cent in all. The 1960 gap of roughly 3⅓ million persons will thus be projected by our methods to over 4 million in 1970. The rest of the 1970 gap of 7.7 million between our projections and those of the NPA arises from the time-pattern of employment growth and the 1960 discrepancy between their projections and the actual level of employment.

THE RAPIDITY OF CHANGE

A matter of considerable interest at the present time is the rapidity of technical change. In particular, it is frequently asked whether the pace of change is accelerating. As we have observed, the projected rates of change of most job groups lie between those of the forties and fifties. We can, however, derive more detailed information from our data and estimate the number of jobs gained or lost by the changing industrial job structure.

Changes in the output of an industry reflect some average change in product per worker, and the NPA projections were themselves based on some estimates of future movements of such measures of productivity. Output per man may be increased at a certain rate when all workers are considered, but shifts also occur in the input coefficients of the various job families and job-content levels employed. Productivity, as usually measured, may be increasing rapidly for blue-collar sections of the labor force, but not nearly so fast for managerial and clerical workers. Differing growth rates of "productivity" will simply reflect the substitution of one job group for another. Such changes in the relative input coefficients of different types of labor are one aspect of technical change.

It is within this framework that the rapidity of change in job content will be examined. It is assumed that in 1970 total employment in each industry will be as the NPA has projected. However, how many jobs in each cell of the matrix will be "created" or "destroyed" because of changes in relative input coefficients within each industry? To answer the question posed earlier, we can compare such figures with similar estimates for the 1950's.

In brief, the method employed starts with the 1950 job-content matrices by industry and the total growth of each industry's employment to 1960. From this is derived an estimate of 1960 job content in the absence of internal change by simply multiplying the 1950 matrices by the decennial growth factors. What results is an estimate of employment shifts due purely to changes in the industrial composition of the economy. Differences between numbers so derived and actual employment in 1960 reflect the creation or destruction of jobs because of internal changes in job content within industries. The same procedure can be applied to the estimates of 1970 by multiplying the 1960 job-content matrices by the 1970 employment relatives shown in Table 21. The estimated employment gains or losses are shown in detail in Table 40 of Appendix III. The United States totals are given in Table 30.

From 1950 to 1960 some 20,000 jobs were created by the shift toward the occupations with the highest job-content level—about one third of the num-

Table 30. Employment effects of intra-industry changes in job-content shares, by job-content level, 1950–1970.

(thousands)

Level	1950–1960	1960–1970
I	20	63
II	1268	1492
III	−22	−169
IV	−476	−238
V	−954	−1029

ber projected for the coming decade. The 1950's saw a net creation of about 1,270,000 level II jobs in the same fashion, while our 1970 projections call for roughly 1.5 million in this category. Similarly, in the past decade about 20,000 level III jobs were lost because of relative input shifts, and some 170,000 will be lost in the sixties. This source of decline in level IV jobs is projected to diminish from about 475,000 to 240,000 in the coming decade, while the effect of input shifts on bottom-level jobs will rise from a loss of 950,000 to one of 1,030,000. On this aggregate level, then, we seem to have uncovered a prediction of a more rapid shift because of internal changes in industries than that which occurred in the decade after 1950.

On the level of the individual job family, the changes in comparison with recent experience yield further information about the rate of technical change. For the most part, the losses of jobs due to relative changes in labor input coefficients in the blue-collar groups are expected to be greater in the sixties. Both the tool and the machine and equipment job families show this tendency clearly. Inspection family jobs will probably gain from these shifts at a somewhat accelerated rate, and the same is true of clerical, personal services, and research jobs. Level II administrative jobs will gain more rapidly, and the other levels will lose more rapidly, from these intra-industrial changes than they did in the fifties. Reversals of direction are forecast for only one job family—protection, which goes from a small loss to a net gain. All other job families will tend to experience much the same changes as in the previous decade.

SUMMARY

A set of estimates of 1970 job content was created depending on a simple assumption about intra-industry changes in job distributions. On the aggregate level, these estimates forecast a continued increase in the share of the higher and medium levels of job content and a continued trend toward homogeneity among the regions of the country. The weaknesses of these projections were carefully noted. These data forecast rates of growth for most job families and job-content levels which lie between the extremes of previous experience. It was also seen that the employment effects of intra-industry shifts in relative input coefficients were projected to be generally larger than those of the 1950's.

Chapter 5

IMPLICATIONS OF THE PROJECTIONS: EMPLOYMENT AND TRAINING ADJUSTMENTS TO 1970

The ease of accomplishing the changing job content predicted in Chapter 4 varies widely from one part of the matrix to another. The magnitude of the adjustments involved can be assessed in two ways: by a comparison with the historical shifts of the past two decades, or in terms of some age and training characteristics of the jobs involved. The first will yield a rough indication of the responsiveness of the particular job group to variations in the buoyancy of aggregate demand, and hence a rough measure of the amount of "natural" mobility which might be expected. It was shown in Chapter 4 that most groups in the job-content matrix are projected to grow at rates between those of the past two decades. In these cases we seem to have reasonable evidence of the attainability of the 1970 forecasts; the exceptions to this pattern, however, require further examination. The second (more intensive) method of analysis will give us better information about the difficulty in achieving the more extreme adjustments.

AGE DISTRIBUTION AND ADAPTABILITY

The age distribution of a job group or occupation will yield considerable information about its adaptability to change. Age distribution influences adaptation and movement in three principal ways. In the first place, there will of course be greater attrition from an occupation dominated by elderly workers (due to death or retirement) than from an occupation dominated by youthful workers. A large percentage of young workers means lower losses from such causes, but implies a higher degree of retrainability and turnover, because of trial jobs, family formation, and geographical movement. Third, some occupations are primarily transitory in an individual's occupational life cycle, and one should therefore expect considerable turnover.

In the case of a job group which is slated to undergo large aggregate losses in the next ten years, the distribution of its members by age will indicate a great deal about the ease with which these losses can be absorbed. In the first case, we must inquire what proportion of workers will probably die, retire, or otherwise leave the occupation. In the second case, the adaptability of the group may depend in large measure on the proportion of younger workers, since the ability and desire to change jobs or undergo retraining seems to be concentrated among those under twenty-five years of age. In this context the President's Manpower Report related that, in 1961, only 4 per cent of workers aged fifty-five to sixty-four changed jobs, and only 10 per cent of those thirty-five to forty-four. On the other hand, workers aged eighteen to twenty-four had a job-changing rate of 25 per cent.[1] Similarly, in 1963 roughly 30 per cent of all the trainees under the Manpower Development and Training Act and Area Redevelopment Act programs were less than twenty-two years old, and the proportion of male trainees in this age group was even higher.

The concentration of employees into these two age extremes should thus give us a very rough measure of adaptability to employment decreases. Somewhat the same thing holds true for projected sharp increases. A fairly high proportion of older workers will compound any problems associated with a sharp increase in employment.

This type of analysis is not exhaustive, but simply indicative of one aspect of adaptability. Use of a fuller form of analysis is clearly limited by the data and knowledge available at the present. We know little about the lifetime patterns of job-holding and the process of change as it relates to the age of the worker and his occupational affiliation. It is recognized of course that certain occupations are "primary" and others are "transitory" or "secondary," in the sense that they represent qualitatively different rungs on the occupational ladder. Primary occupations are those about which a man's lifetime career is likely to be centered. Secondary occupations are often temporary or transitional: they may be taken up in preparation for a primary occupation or upon retirement from one.

For example, few people presumably take on the occupation of farm laborer with permanent status in mind. In this case, the job is often summer employment, or the workers plan to become farmers later on. Occupations which are usually classed as professional or managerial tend to be more uniformly "primary," with many of the laborer and operative jobs being (at least in original intent) way-stations. Workers tend to enter and leave farm labor early in life, to enter and leave the self-employed managerial class late, and to enter the professions fairly early and leave them quite late. There are furthermore some occupations which tend to be held by those who have retired from their primary occupations.[2] These considerations impose caution on the simple use of age distribution as an index of adaptability. People working as small shopkeepers, for instance, may be very elderly, but there may be no reason for the group to appear any younger at the next census. Nevertheless, one should be able to get an idea of the number of people who must leave an occupation in the next decade, or who will respond best to retraining from a study of the age distribution.

The importance of such studies of the characteristics of employment, entry, and exit for various industries has been emphasized by Dunlop.[3] An example of what he has termed an industry Manpower Profile was developed for the railroads in connection with the work of the Presidential Railroad Commission. This was an attempt to survey the characteristics of workers in an industry faced with long-term declining employment. From better knowledge of this sort, more appropriate policy solutions can be formulated. Such detailed studies would be as valuable on a job-content basis as they are on an industry basis.

Problems for several job groups. As can be seen from Table 39 of Appendix III, there are certain job groups whose behavior is not expected to resemble closely that which went before. In these cases, such as the specialized tool job family, deeper inquiry must be made. For example, job-content level II of this family is expected to decline in the next decade by 11.4 per cent. The ease with which this decline will come about depends to some extent on the natural losses we can expect. In this case, some 5.1 per cent of those employed in 1960 were over sixty-five years of age, and 10.7 per cent were over sixty. If the preponderance of the 10.7 per cent leave the job group in the coming ten years—not an unjustified assumption—then approximately three quarters of the expected net loss can come from this source. Since only 2.2 per cent of the workers were over seventy in 1960, we should be able to count on 8.5 per cent of the work force leaving because of death or retirement in the age group over sixty years of age.

In this case, because of the high ratio of elderly workers in 1960 to the projected rate of job loss, it does not seem likely that the transitional problems will be too great. But, to further buttress the argument, this job group had a very high percentage of younger workers in 1960. This is likely to be the group most easily diverted to growing job groups either by natural mobility or by retraining and other policies. Eleven per cent of the workers were between the ages of fourteen and twenty-four, and almost one quarter were between fourteen and twenty-nine. In addition, the presence of a large number of younger workers implies that adjustments can be carried out (either by conscious policies or through market forces) by discouraging the entrance of new workers. In summary, although a sharp reduction of employment in this job group has been forecast, it should be accompanied by difficulties of a smaller order of magnitude than if the age distribution were different.

Similarly, the problems posed by the projected 2.3 per cent decline in level II of the vehicle operation family will be more concerned with the level of gross entry rather than with the need for workers to leave the group involuntarily. In 1960 18.9 per cent of the workers were over sixty, but only 1.2 per cent were over seventy. Thus about six times the projected net loss should occur easily through the attrition implied by the elderly age distribution of this group.

As a further example, consider a large pool of relatively lower or unskilled job content, whose general similarities in terms of job requirements should permit joint analysis. Levels IV and V of the four tool and machine families have been projected to decline collectively by about 1 per cent from 1960 to 1970. In most of these groups, the number over sixty years of age is a fair-sized fraction of the total 1960–1970 adjustment. Also, in many cases the percentage of youthful workers is fairly high (which implies better than average prospects for mobility and retraining). If the seven job groups as a whole can be regarded as drawing their workers from a single broad pool of abilities and skills, then the adaptability of the total group to the small aggregate changes forecast should be quite high. Eight per cent of the workers were over sixty, and about one quarter were younger than twenty-nine. Viewed solely in the light of the effects of the job decline on the persons presently employed who may not wish to leave their present jobs, the prospects are good for a smooth adjustment in this broad range of the work force. However, prospects for new entry are clearly quite poor.

On the other hand, examples can be adduced where the age distribution will exacerbate already sizable net-inflow requirements. Level I of the clerical job family was projected to increase by 43.6 per cent in the coming decade. Another 8.5 per cent will probably be required to replace those who leave because of age. Another effect on the total number of entrants required can be seen in level III of the same family, but this time due to the peculiar age-sex combination. An increase of 30.9 per cent was predicted, and over one fifth of this group consists of women between fourteen and twenty-nine years of age. Presumably, many of them will have to be replaced in the next ten years. This will augment the training requirements associated with the large net increase projected for the group.

It must be emphasized that these estimates are quite speculative, looking only at the numbers employed in 1960 at either end of the age spectrum. To be able to make firm predictions of the adaptability of the various job groups and broad regions of job content, further data are required. As yet we know little of the turnover rates of each occupation. More data on the migration from job group to job group, retirements, and even mortality rates for different occupations would be required for a proper and thorough study.

LEVELS OF EDUCATION AND TRAINING REQUIREMENTS

Changing levels of educational and training requirements are an important consequence of economic and technical change. Mention has already been made of effects on the technical foci of training stemming from the changing importance of various job families. At this point, estimates can be presented of the average levels of general and specific training required by the jobs in our economy. The estimates are based on the data found in *Worker Traits*

Characteristics for 4000 Jobs and the school-year equivalents earlier proposed by Richard S. Eckaus.[4]

Estimates of general educational development and specific vocational preparation for the 90 cells of the job-content matrix were presented in Tables 7 and 8 of Chapter 2. If the values there shown for each cell are assumed constant over time, estimates can easily be made for level changes due to differing growth patterns within the matrix. Such estimates are given in Table 31. Since data on educational and training requirements were developed only for jobs in the 1949 *Dictionary of Occupational Titles*, it is impossible to assess any shifts arising from changing requirements for individual jobs.

These estimates show a continued gradual rise in required levels of both general education and specific training. Although changes in the relative importance of various cells have caused most of the averages to decline when computed across content levels, the continuous rise in the over-all level of

Table 31. General educational development and specific vocational preparation requirements, and job-content levels, 1940–1970.

Level	Number of years required for general educational development			
	1940	1950	1960	1970
Total	9.99	10.14	10.37	10.49
I	16.31	16.21	16.17	16.11
II	12.01	12.04	12.11	12.17
III	10.54	10.50	10.46	10.43
IV	9.75	9.63	9.48	9.43
V	7.85	7.89	7.93	7.96

Level	Number of years required for specific vocational preparation			
	1940	1950	1960	1970
Total	1.78	1.82	1.86	1.88
I	5.40	5.30	5.27	5.23
II	3.21	3.19	3.18	3.19
III	1.92	1.82	1.63	1.49
IV	1.40	1.29	1.12	1.03
V	.82	.81	.80	.79

job content has led to increased mean national requirements. The required level of general educational development rose 1.5 per cent from 1940 to 1950, and 2.3 per cent from 1950 to 1960. Mean specific vocational preparation requirements rose by 2.2 per cent in both decades. The projections of Chapter 4 do not indicate an accelerated rate of increase, but precisely the opposite. The rates at which mean GED and SVP requirements rose during the fifties are expected to be halved in the present decade. Mean GED is expected to rise by 1.2 per cent to 1970, and mean SVP by 1.1 per cent. These percentage increases are equivalent to rises of about six and one-half weeks and one week of training time for GED and SVP respectively. The comparable increases during the decade from 1950 to 1960 were twelve weeks and four weeks.

The changing sources of training. Any attempt to survey the implications of the projections for training and the allocation of training resources is hindered by lack of appropriate data. Ideally, one could estimate the exact training requirements of the job structure of 1970, compare it with that of 1960, estimate attrition, and arrive at estimates of the amount and type of training required.

Not only are there conceptual difficulties involved in the quantification of training, but the only available data are rather sketchy. The 1964 Manpower Report published some new data on source of training reported from a sample of the employment records.[5] Data are presented for about 80 of the 200-odd occupations that have been used elsewhere in this study. For this reason, the discussion that follows must be incomplete and based only on further estimates that can be made from these data.

The reported sources of workers' training for their current jobs are broken down into four groups. The first, "formal training," includes schools, apprenticeship programs, and training in the armed forces. The second group, "on the job," contains those who learned in company training programs or who reached their present position through promotion. "Casual training," the third category, comprises those who learned from relatives or friends, or who replied that they "just picked up" the job. The fourth group, those who replied that no training was needed, is fairly self-explanatory. There is some doubt whether the present grouping displays the data in the most useful manner, and whether the categories are very meaningful. A system by which 13 per cent of the unpaid farm family workers are listed as having learned their job by formal means (as did over 10 per cent of the private household workers), while 28 per cent of the noncollege

Table 32. Ways in which workers learned their current job, by job-content levels: April 1963.

(per cent)

| Level | Number reporting | | | |
	Formal	On the job	Casual	No training needed
Total[a]	30.2	56.2	45.4	7.5
I	56	71	32	3
II	55	68	39	2
III	46	62	38	3
IV	20	51	48	11
V	9	42	50	16

[a] Calculated by Department of Labor from its sample. The totals of the 4 columns for any content level do not equal 100 since many workers reported more than one source of training.

Table 33. Ways in which workers learned their current jobs, by job family: April 1963.

(per cent)

Job family	Formal	On the job	Casual	No training needed
Total	30.2	56.2	45.4	7.5
Tools	41	57	49	2
Machines	12	60	41	4
Inspection	54	83	30	2
Vehicle operation	13	47	52	12
Farm	20	17	78	8
Sales A	42	74	39	2
Sales B	19	59	49	8
Clerical	59	70	25	1
Protection	42	79	29	2
Personal services	10	34	50	18
Entertainment	—[a]	—[a]	—[a]	—[a]
Health	74	52	25	3
Education	56	42	28	7
Welfare	—[a]	—[a]	—[a]	—[a]
Admin. & org.	36	54	58	4
Research & design	71	81	33	1

[a] Base too small to allow estimates for the job families.

teachers learned their job "casually," and a further 7 per cent said no training was required, poses its own questions.

Nevertheless, a summary of the results in the format of job content is presented in Tables 32 and 33. The percentage distributions given in the Manpower Report were simply averaged over the job-content levels in Table 32, and over job families in Table 33: the weakness of the data made a weighted average seem unnecessarily exact. Also, as estimates were given for only 85 census occupations, the data cannot usefully be presented in matrix form.

These data generally bear out our expectations—a direct relationship between the level of job content and the percentage attributing their training to formal or on-the-job procedures. Similarly, those who picked up their training casually or said none was required are more important at the lower and unskilled job-content levels. The implications of such a pattern, in the light of the projected changes in job structure to 1970, are fairly clear. On the conservative assumption that the source distribution of each aggregate content level does not change, a 1970 distribution for the United States can be estimated. The employment estimates of Chapter 4 would be accompanied by the following source distribution: formal training, 35.4 per cent; on-the-job training, 57.3 per cent; casual training, 42.2 per cent; no training required, 7.2 per cent. This serves to depict the broad outlines of the problem before us, and emphasizes the projected rise in formal training requirements.

The estimates of Table 33 reveal sizable differences among job families in the sources of training. The most rapidly growing job families tend also to be the ones with the greatest emphasis on formal sources. Inspection, clerical, health, and research and design job families were all projected to grow by over 30 per cent in the 1960's, and all four have high levels of formal training. The only exception is the family of personal service jobs, which may grow rapidly, but has very low formal and on-the-job requirements.

One further aspect of the training problem must be mentioned which cannot be discussed with reference to these data. The sources of training reported were given by workers for only their *current* jobs. They therefore are not in any sense an inventory of the training capabilities of the labor force. Discussions of automation frequently stress that workers will have to be able to change jobs two or three times more often in the course of a lifetime. Data representing the inventory of training would have to be developed to analyze this assertion and its implications.

The sex composition of employment. It was noticed in Chapter 3 that the

Table 34. Projections of the labor force to 1970: male and female.

Level	Decennial rates of growth		Male share
	Male	*Female*	
Total	15.8	26.3	65.6
I	31.1	26.4	66.3
II	35.4	38.4	89.2
III	16.4	28.6	60.6
IV	2.6	28.1	64.7
V	3.8	20.5	57.4

employment patterns and changes of the sexes over the past twenty years have differed widely. If it is assumed that the sex breakdown of each cell of the content matrix will be the same in 1970 as it was in 1960, projections by sex can be developed from the data of Table 26, Chapter 4. For example, if in 1960, 80 per cent of the clerical workers at content level III were women, then we assume that 80 per cent will be women in 1970, and derive the actual numerical estimates from the data of Chapter 4. These estimates are summarized in Table 34, which shows rates of growth by sex and job-content levels and the projected male share in 1970.

These figures portray a continuation of past trends—the jobs that will grow more rapidly have large percentages of women. Women's share of total employment and at all job-content levels except level I will expand in the coming decade. Many new women's jobs will appear in the sales, clerical,

Table 35. Labor force, employment, and rates of unemployment by sex: 1960 and 1970.

Category	1960	1970
Labor force (millions):		
Male	49.5	56.3
Female	23.6	29.4
Employment (millions):		
Male	44.5	53.1
Female	21.2	27.8
Unemployment rate:		
Male	5.1	5.7
Female	5.9	5.4

Source: Monthly Labor Review, October 1962, pp. 1089–1099; April 1964, p. 462.

and service job families. Although women's employment will grow much more rapidly than men's, the differential should be narrower than it was from 1950 to 1960.

This pattern of growth will tend to change the unemployment positions of the sexes. If the NPA-projected total employment of 80.9 million is achieved in 1970, the distributions of Table 34 imply that about 53 million will be male. These estimates can be compared with projections of the 1970 labor force by sex prepared by the Bureau of Labor Statistics. The relevant figures, shown in Table 35, project a reversal of the 1960 situation in which the male unemployment rate was the lower of the two. The type of growth that we have projected above, with no changes in the sex composition of occupations, would lead to a continued worsening of the male unemployment problem, although the female situation would improve somewhat.

SUMMARY

This chapter has looked more closely at some of the changes involved in the projections to 1970. It was seen that, in some cases, the movements arising from natural attrition and the higher levels of mobility associated with youthful workers appeared sufficient to meet problems of adjustment. In other cases, the age pattern might simply augment the task of adjustment required by the projections. The pattern of growth projected for the job-content matrix was seen to imply an increase, at a reduced rate, in the levels of general education and specific training requirements and a shift toward the greater importance of more formal training procedures. Jobs with casual training or requiring none at all would continue to decline in importance. A continuation of the 1960 sex breakdown within job groups was seen to indicate a worsened unemployment situation for males in 1970.

The 1970 projections, however, were intended only to suggest the magnitude of changes that may occur. It is therefore not in these implications that the main value and conclusion of this chapter must lie. Rather, we can infer that the concept and method of quantifying job content are of considerable use in the analysis of the implications of changing job patterns.

Chapter 6

SUMMARY AND CONCLUSIONS

At least since the time of Adam Smith, economists have been concerned with the different and changing nature of work. The historical and anticipated influences of capital accumulation and technological change have been an important part of this concern. Monotony and drudgery were often said to characterize the emerging jobs, although writers did not usually recognize the full complexity of the changes involved. It has been the purpose of this study to develop a model of the nature of jobs performed and to apply this model to an empirical analysis of the United States economy.

Goals and procedures. For the analysis of the effects of technological and market change upon the types of jobs in an economy, an appropriate model of job content is required. Two dimensions of occupational structure were examined in Chapter 2 which describe important facets of the problem. In the first place, the content of a job is clearly dependent upon its technical focus—the major equipment or function about which the job is centered. On this basis, the job-family dimension was developed, in which each job family corresponds with a major technical focus which answers the question: what does the holder of the job do? The second relevant dimension of the structure—the relative levels of job content—was analogous to the problems of job evaluation. It was recognized that job-content level depends on a wide range of factors, among which are skill, responsibility, and the complexity of the job performed.

These job families which describe important aspects of job content are connected in principle with the underlying fabric of economic and industrial life. Within a plant or unit of operation, there exist clusters or families of jobs centered about a machine, process, or department and connected with patterns of wages and of labor movement. Differing educational and training requirements are associated with the various clusters and the jobs within them. The job families on the aggregate level are the analogue of those found on the level of the plant. Many of their characteristics should also be analogous, for example, with respect to wage structure, education, and training requirements, and patterns of labor promotion and movement.

Nevertheless, the nature of the presently available data does not permit the construction of economy-wide estimates of job families by directly aggregating those which could be observed at the workplace. The census data apply to broad occupations or groups of occupations, and fall far short of describing the myriad jobs in an industrial economy. For this reason, attempts to describe the job-family aspect of job content must proceed in a more deductive fashion. It was necessary to identify useful families within the range of total employment in the context of the questions about changing job content and within the confines of available data. An experimental set of job families was derived by this method, which seemed to maximize the information obtained from the census detail. The placing of census occupations into these families was based upon factors of technical focus, patterns of mobility, and the substitutability and transferability of the jobs and abilities involved. Census titles were placed into five levels of job content (I–V) partially on the basis of a regression analysis of income, training requirements, and aptitutes required by component jobs. The regression coefficients were viewed as estimates of the market values of various skills and abilities, and occupations were evaluated using these weights. The process was not, however, followed mechanically, because problems with the scope and accuracy of the requirement and aptitude data require the use of judgment based on outside information.

The changing content of jobs. On the basis of the principles of job families and of job evaluation, the experimental model of job content was applied to the United States. Arrayed in this fashion, the data show wide differences by region, industry, and sex. Furthermore, over the past twenty years considerable changes have occurred in the job family and content-level distributions of the United States. That many of these changes can be expected to continue was the general implication of the projections prepared for 1970. The period from 1940 to 1960 witnessed large growth in the upper three levels of job content at the expense of the lower two. There were also substantial differences in the behavior of the various job families. Blue-collar and farm families declined; white-collar service and inspection jobs showed strong growth. The effect of changes in industrial composition and different rates of growth was to produce greater similarity among the regional job-content mixes. Rates of growth by sex also differed—with women accounting for an increasing share of additions in employment. Content-level distributions also differ widely by sex, and do not seem to be moving toward greater similarity.

Our projections were based upon National Planning Association (NPA) industry estimates for 1970 and the 1950–1960 intra-industry changes in job structure. It was felt that such procedures yielded a reasonable range for estimates of 1970 consistent with past experience. This method projects a continued homogenization of job content between regions and continued increasing importance of higher and moderate job-content levels. Past shifts toward white-collar service and inspection jobs would be continued or accentuated. If the 1960 sex distributions for job groups are applied to the 1970 figures, the unemployment situation by sex breakdown is projected to become more unfavorable for males. The estimates imply a move toward somewhat higher levels of education and training requirements and greater importance of more formal training procedures.

Past changes in job content have been associated with the buoyancy of aggregate demand, and many projected changes fit within the range of historical experience. A preliminary analysis was made of some groups which might undergo sharply different behavior. It is in this area that the need for better data is most evident. Better information about type, length, and source of training is needed to appraise training requirements. Increased knowledge of retirement patterns and interjob mobility is necessary to assess the problems of movement involved in a changing economy. The concept and methods of job-content analysis can serve to identify the major areas of concern and the types of jobs involved, but the full requirements posed by the 1970 projections call for more complete data.

The need for new data forms. Contrasts were drawn between the goals of measuring job content and the purposes of the most prevalent occupational data—the social-economic groups. The latter were not devised to reflect the structure of job content in our economy, and must therefore be of less value in studies of education and training, wage structure, and mobility. These groupings do not reflect accurately the technical foci of jobs, nor do they consistently indicate relative levels of job content. One of the express purposes of the social-economic classes was to ignore the actual work performed and stress the status of the occupation.

Another type of job classification has been designed by Sidney A. Fine, primarily with placement problems in mind. This system is based on the level and orientation of jobs with respect to data, people, and things. Aside from the conceptual and methodological difficulties in this system, it conceals important information about the technical content of the work performed. Indeed, the method of "functional job analysis" is supposed to cut through the "terminologies" of specific technologies. However, with regard to worker movement in internal and external labor markets, training requirements, and the problems of worker placement, the specific technology and the focus of the job are generally extremely important. Knowledge of the position of a job on a ladder of promotion is clearly essential to a successful placement program. Furthermore, the fact that many jobs are acquired by upward movement along a promotion line implies that training requirements may not be best defined simply with respect to the entry job, but to the type of skills, abilities, and training characteristics in the over-all family of jobs. Entry requirements are generally not the minimum required for the job itself, but reflect the content of jobs at higher levels. Such information related to the structure and operation of labor markets is suppressed by Fine's concept of functional job analysis.

Our ability to deduce theoretically useful and proper job families was limited by the available data. The detailed information from the census was employed in empirical estimates of job content (since these are the only existing data). Even the finest detail is on a broad enough basis to limit considerably the subdivision of the job structure into families. Also, important questions referring to the production-maintenance job distribution and the relation of the worker to the machine could not be answered, since the data do not reflect these distinctions.

For these reasons, one of the purposes of this study was to indicate new ways of gathering and presenting data. This general problem should be dealt with on two levels: the type of basic detailed data to be collected, and the goals and methods of aggregating such data. An attempt has been made to develop a scheme of data presentation which reveals important aspects of job content. It was argued that job content is reflected by the family or major technical focus of the various jobs, and the relative levels of job content. To study problems associated with market and technological change, the aggregate data should be presented in a form similar to that employed in this volume. To perform this task more successfully, fuller data on the characteristics of jobs are required to allow the construction of a more narrowly defined set of job families and content levels.

The ease with which this will be done and the reliability and usefulness of the resulting aggregates depend to a large extent on the nature of the basic detailed data. In the first place, to evaluate patterns of change and to facilitate projection, basic job data should certainly be collected more frequently than at the present ten-year intervals. Data should also be collected for a greater number of more homogeneous, clearly defined jobs, rather than the present broad occupations. Job data have the further virtue that they are easily transferable to other schemes of aggregation. To eliminate much of the need for broad occupational definitions and to obtain more informed responses, these data might be collected from establishments or firms, rather than from households as at present. This was the conclusion of the President's Committee to Appraise Employment and Unemployment Statistics, but the six years since that report have seen little research on the feasibility or accuracy of such an approach. The BLS industry wage surveys, which cover a fair proportion of the labor force in better detail than the census, should be considered as a possible part of a program of expanded data.

That a procedure to gain information on specific jobs should be explored is emphasized by the supplementary data which already exist on this basis. "Worker Traits" in terms of schooling and specialized training, skills, aptitudes, temperaments, and other factors reflecting job content have already been developed for some 4000 of the jobs in the *Dictionary*, and supplemented by additional information in the third edition. With employment data collected on this basis, the identification of job families and job-content levels for the whole economy could be more fully developed and more firmly based. These data would also assist in the construction of a set of broad job groupings which, although not revealing some information yielded by the full set of job families, could be used to collect data on a more frequent basis (such as quarterly or monthly samples).

The value of a system of job families and content levels to study the changing job content of the American economy has been demonstrated above. Such a system will be useful for analysis of education and training, problems of wage structure, and the study of labor movement and mobility. The major bar to the development of this measure of job content lies in the broadness of census occupational data and the lack of numerical information on the relevant criteria for job evaluation. This problem can only be met by a more detailed classification, in which the basic unit is the job—not the vague, technically imprecise concept of an occupation—and where job characteristics are measured less in terms of aptitude and temperament, and more in conformity with the customary concepts of job evaluation.

The theory and measurement of job content—perspective. The final question arising from this study concerns the generality of the approach employed. The macro-economic conception of job families and job-content levels corresponds to the realities of the workplace, and could theoretically be measured by summing the specific job families and clusters found there. Nevertheless, we must still inquire: how general is this approach; to what extent is the framework of job content appropriate to questions relating to the work people do?

At first glance, it does not seem that the job-content approach has any claim to greater generality or broader usefulness than any other system. Although we have emphasized that the present social-economic groups do not form the proper analytical vehicle for modern manpower research, there still may exist legitimate curiosity about the class structure of our society. Social strata do not appear in the format of job content. Nor could we study directly the impact of tariff reductions on various kinds of jobs; we should instead use Edward Atkinson's classification of 1903, or a modern version developed for this purpose. More generally, the data and classification schemes employed must have been created with a particular problem in mind. It would be as great folly to expect social status to be perfectly or simply related to the level of job content as it would be to use the social-economic groups as measures of the kinds of jobs in our economy.

However, both theory and the reality in which it is grounded assure us that a broad range of interrelated problems can fruitfully be studied within the framework of job content. This considerable degree of generality stems from the nature of the basic foundation—the concept of the specific job. The level and nature of education and training required for a job are intimately related to the technical focus and content level of the job. The focus or family will tend to fix the type of training and the content of the courses and programs needed; the level of job content will clearly affect the amount and duration of such training. Aggregate job families and job-content levels are related to the analysis of wage levels and movements, just as their counterparts in the plant or workplace form the basic fabric for the study of compensation there. These same micro-economic families are essential to the study of movement through the internal labor markets of firms, and analogous macro-economic problems can be studied with aggregate families. Both the mobility characteristics and the actual movement of workers will depend on the job family and content level of their jobs. The variables listed here are peculiarly related to the nature and distribution of jobs, while their relation to social-economic status or worker orientation is at best tenuous.

As the concept of a job refers to specific duties and functions characterizing particular worker/work relationships, it is clearly the proper fundamental unit to use in describing the work performed in an economy. The concept of job content, measured by families and content levels, is founded on the natural structuring of jobs at the workplace into clusters and ladders focused on some function, process, or piece of equipment. This structure is directly related to problems of compensation, movement, training, and skill requirements. The success and underlying methodology of the empirical results here presented may be open to question, but the relevance of the concept to the analysis of work performed and a broad set of job-related variables has been sufficiently demonstrated.

APPENDIX I

This appendix (Table 36) contains the allocation of detailed census titles to the families and content levels of the job-content matrix. The code numbers refer to the 1950 *Classified Index of Occupations,* while the three columns at the right present estimates of required General Educational Development (GED), Specific Vocational Preparation (SVP), and finally the value of the job determined as described on pp. 23–27.

Table 36. Allocation of census occupations to job families and content levels.

	Estimates of:		
Job family and level	general education development (years)[a]	specific vocational preparation (years)[a]	"value of the job" based on worker traits characteristics (dollars)
Tools—specialized			
I			
092 Surveyors	15.00	2.62	6724
II			
571 Photoengravers	10.53	4.46	5229
512 Compositors & typesetters	12.00	4.38	5536
543 Loom fixers	10.00	3.00	5132
534 Jewelers	11.53	3.63	5755
572 Piano & organ tuners	12.00	3.00	5869
520 Electrotypers	11.00	5.00	4982
III			
584 Stonecutters	9.89	3.23	5111
501 Blacksmiths	11.18	2.18	5348
573 Plasterers	10.50	2.62	4890
622 Blasters & powdermen	10.50	2.92	4890
540 Linemen & servicemen	10.61	2.18	5242
502 Bookbinders	8.33	3.56	4492
644 Meatcutters, except slaughter house	10.00	2.51	5132
504 Brickmasons	9.73	1.92	4749
525 Furriers	10.67	2.50	4550
582 Shoemakers, except factory	12.40	2.40	4829
645 Milliners	8.71	1.01	4562
671 Photographic process workers	9.40	1.27	4688
581 Roofers and slaters	—	—	—
563 Opticians	8.67	1 49	4212

[a] These estimates were first published in the *Review of Economics and Statistics,* November 1966. Permission to reprint them is gratefully acknowledged.

Table 36. Allocation of census occupations to job families and content levels. (*continued*)

Job family and level	general education development (*years*)	specific vocational preparation (*years*)	"*value of the job*" based on worker traits characteristics (*dollars*)
	Estimates of:		

Tools—specialized (*continued*)

IV

633 Dressmakers, except factory	9.25	2.44	4290
600 Apprentices	11.36	.16	5381
590 Tailors	10.67	1.62	4883
623 Boatmen and canalmen	9.67	2.51	4766
674 Sawyers	8.70	1.08	4588
630 Chainmen, rodmen, and axmen	7.40	.70	4350
670 Painters, except construction	7.15	.75	3562
511 Cement finishers	11.50	2.62	4702
565 Paperhangers	—	—	—

V

643 Laundry operatives	8.42	.63	4166
940 Longshoremen	7.20	.25	4313
950 Lumbermen, raftsmen, & woodchoppers	6.71	.52	3890
634 Dyers	8.86	.96	3875
673 Sailors and deck hands	7.14	1.68	3931

Tools—nonspecialized

I

521 Engravers except photoengravers	11.46	4.08	5770

II

551 Mechanics, office machine	11.00	3.00	5658
554 Mechanics, n.e.c.[b]	11.44	2.83	5766
592 Tool and die makers	11.62	3.78	6143
570 Pattern and model makers	11.47	3.64	6115
560 Millwrights	12.00	3.00	6212
535 Job setters	10.67	3.00	5968
591 Tinsmiths	11.60	2.57	5796
505 Cabinetmakers	12.00	3.00	5508
544 Machinists	11.69	3.32	5441

III

574 Plumbers and pipefitters	11.23	3.83	5728
503 Boilermakers	11.78	2.29	5829

[b] Not elsewhere classified.

Table 36. Allocation of census occupations to job families
and content levels. (*continued*)

| Job family and level | Estimates of: | | |
	general education development (*years*)	specific vocational preparation (*years*)	*"value of the job" based on worker traits characteristics* (*dollars*)
Tools—nonspecialized (*continued*)			
620 Asbestos & insulation workers	12.00	2.25	5869
545 Mechanics, airplane	10.71	2.34	4929
550 Mechanics, automobile	10.80	1.66	4945
552 Mechanics, radio & T.V.	12.00	3.00	5165
561 Molders, metal	9.17	1.71	5017
515 Electricians	11.14	1.73	5007
585 Structural metal workers	9.88	1.47	5147
594 Craftsmen, n.e.c.[b]	10.83	2.32	5284
510 Carpenters	11.67	2.70	5438
553 Mechanics, railroad & car shop	10.00	.75	5132
530 Glaziers	10.00	2.50	4788
564 Painters, construction	10.90	1.78	4592
635 Filers and grinders, metal	8.67	1.16	4926
685 Welders and flame cutters	9.85	.61	4771
IV			
593 Upholsterers	9.00	1.59	3901
662 Oilers & greasers, except automobile	5.60	.33	3687
770 Janitors and sextons	8.29	1.21	4485
V			
920 Garage laborers	2.67	.04	2779
970 Laborers, n.e.c.[b]	6.46	.46	4178
Machines and equipment—specialized			
I			
II			
562 Motion picture projectionists	12.00	3.00	5127
575 Pressmen, printing	10.90	4.19	4963
076 Radio operators	11.60	.74	5796
074 Photographers	12.67	2.01	5260
III			
684 Weavers, textile	12.00	3.00	5498
500 Bakers	9.25	1.54	4318
672 Power station operators	10.30	1.55	5558

[b] Not elsewhere classified.

Table 36. Allocation of census occupations to job families
and content levels. (*continued*)

Job family and level	Estimates of:		
	general education development (*years*)	specific vocational preparation (*years*)	"value of the job" based on worker traits characteristics (*dollars*)
Machines and equipment—specialized (*continued*)			
642 Heaters, metal	—	—	—
522 Excavating machine operators	8.88	.82	4593
IV			
675 Spinners, textile	8.00	1.25	4803
555 Millers, grain, etc.	9.22	.97	4655
650 Mine operatives	7.89	1.02	4783
910 Fishermen and oystermen	8.10	.60	4478
V			
Machines and equipment—nonspecialized			
I			
II			
III			
583 Stationary engineers	11.11	2.08	5706
580 Rollers and roll hands	7.90	1.02	4441
513 Cranemen	9.11	.74	5006
IV			
641 Furnacemen	9.94	1.42	4444
524 Forgemen and hammermen	10.33	1.50	4859
531 Heat treaters	10.50	2.13	4176
680 Stationary firemen	11.00	2.25	4982
V			
690 Operatives, n.e.c.[b]	8.56	.98	4191
Inspection			
I			
II			
523 Foremen, n.e.c.[b]	11.70	3.90	5814
095 Technicians, testing	12.27	1.65	5510
III			
533 Inspectors, n.e.c.[b]	11.88	3.58	5476

[b] Not elsewhere classified.

Table 36. Allocation of census occupations to job families
and content levels. (*continued*)

Job family and level	Estimates of:		
	general education development (years)	*specific vocational preparation (years)*	*"value of the job" based on worker traits characteristics (dollars)*
Inspection (*continued*)			
096 Technicians, n.e.c.[b]	12.25	1.76	5544
210 Inspectors, public administration	11.46	2.16	5056
IV			
532 Inspectors, log & lumber	10.64	1.55	4573
V			
640 Fruit graders, except factory	7.00	.21	3905
Vehicle operation			
I			
II			
002 Airplane pilots	—	—	—
240 Officers, ship	11.40	3.53	5388
203 Conductors, railroad	11.00	5.00	5315
541 Locomotive engineers	10.00	2.02	4798
III			
625 Bus drivers	12.00	.75	5498
632 Deliverymen	10.75	1.78	5640
660 Motormen, mine	9.75	.93	4753
322 Dispatchers	11.50	1.97	5434
682 Taxi drivers	9.50	3.52	5040
631 Conductors, bus	—	—	—
542 Locomotive firemen	10.00	.75	4455
683 Truck & tractor drivers	8.50	.25	4895
IV			
960 Teamsters	8.50	.24	4180
681 Switchmen, railroad	7.00	.21	4286
661 Motormen, street railway	—	—	—
V			
621 Attendants, auto service	11.00	1.69	6029
624 Brakemen, railroad	4.00	.00	3393
304 Baggagemen, transportation	—	—	—

[b] Not elsewhere classified.

Table 36. Allocation of census occupations to job families and content levels. (*continued*)

Job family and level	*Estimates of:*		
	general education development (years)	*specific vocational preparation (years)*	*"value of the job" based on worker traits characteristics (dollars)*
Farm			
I			
II			
123 Farm managers	16.00	7.00	6231
III			
810 Farm foremen	12.00	3.00	5498
IV			
100 Farmers	10.67	2.00	4540
840 Farm serv. laborers, self-employed	9.00	1.06	4615
V			
820 Farm laborers, wage workers	8.47	1.20	4175
830 Farm laborers, unpaid family	6.87	.80	3548
Sales A—considerable knowledge of product required			
I			
200 Buyers and department heads, store	16.00	7.00	6592
II			
280 Purchasing agents	12.00	7.00	5117
400 Advertising agents	10.00	.04	5159
450 Insurance agents	10.70	1.19	4917
480 Stock and bond brokers	—	—	—
470 Real estate agents	—	—	—
205 Floormen & managers, store	—	—	—
III			
342 Shipping and receiving clerks	10.00	.75	5132
201 Buyers and shippers, farm	8.00	1.00	4470
IV			
V			
Sales B—little knowledge of product required			
I			
II			
III			
420 Demonstrators	12.00	.16	5526

Table 36. Allocation of census occupations to job families
and content levels. (*continued*)

Job family and level	Estimates of:		
	general education development (years)	*specific vocational preparation (years)*	*"value of the job" based on worker traits characteristics (dollars)*
Sales B—little knowledge of product required (*continued*)			
514 Decorators, window dressers	9.38	.83	3971
IV			
490 Salesmen, n.e.c.[b]	9.12	.82	4970
410 Auctioneers	—	—	—
V			
460 Newsboys	8.50	.04	4551
430 Hucksters and peddlers	6.00	.08	3722
Clerical workers			
I			
000 Accountants and auditors	16.00	5.00	6582
056 Librarians	16.00	5.00	6259
II			
204 Credit men	—	—	—
301 Assistants, library	14.00	3.88	5522
III			
370 Telephone operators	10.86	.63	5317
365 Telegraph operators	9.10	1.06	5086
350 Stenographers, secretaries, typists	10.91	1.58	4993
341 Office machine operators	8.42	.23	4870
310 Bookkeepers	10.33	.44	5553
380 Ticket agents	10.00	.56	5159
305 Bank tellers	—	—	—
300 Agents, n.e.c.[b]	11.73	1.48	4772
390 Clerical workers, n.e.c.[b]	10.22	.79	4829
IV			
321 Collectors, bill	12.00	.04	5183
335 Mail carriers	8.50	.10	4523
320 Cashiers	10.67	.53	4568
325 Express messengers and mail clerks	7.00	.10	3534
V			
360 Telegraph messengers	8.50	.04	4885
340 Messengers and office boys	7.50	.10	4368

[b] Not elsewhere classified.

Table 36. Allocation of census occupations to job families
and content levels. (*continued*)

Job family and level	Estimates of:		
	general education development (*years*)	specific vocational preparation (*years*)	"value of the job" based on worker traits characteristics (*dollars*)
Personal service			
I			
II			
III			
740 Barbers, beauticians	11.00	.94	4611
754 Cooks, except private household	11.33	3.58	4699
764 Housekeepers, except household	11.90	2.23	5137
IV			
731 Attendants, personal service, n.e.c.[b]	8.00	.10	4127
760 Counter workers	7.75	.12	4043
700 Housekeepers, private household	12.00	.94	4822
752 Boardinghouse keepers	12.00	.94	4822
930 Gardeners	7.50	.37	3997
761 Elevator operators	7.00	.04	4276
V			
720 Private household workers, n.e.c.[b]	8.90	.96	4254
790 Service workers, n.e.c.[b]	7.11	.26	4297
750 Bartenders	7.00	.16	4239
780 Porters	4.75	.04	3864
753 Charwomen and cleaners	6.00	.40	3732
710 Laundresses	7.00	.04	3572
784 Waiters	7.00	.61	4276
751 Bootblacks	4.00	.04	2679
Entertainment			
I			
004 Artists	14.80	4.95	5983
057 Musicians and music teachers	16.00	8.67	6259
II			
006 Authors	17.33	1.50	6170
III			
001 Actors	14.00	3.00	5226
031 Dancers and dancing teachers	13.00	3.88	5348
005 Athletes	—	—	—

[b] Not elsewhere classified.

Table 36. Allocation of census occupations to job families
and content levels. (*continued*)

Job family and level	Estimates of:		
	general education development (*years*)	specific vocational preparation (*years*)	"*value of the job*" based on worker traits characteristics (*dollars*)
Entertainment (*continued*)			
IV			
051 Entertainers, n.e.c.[b]	7.00	.38	3201
V			
732 Attendants, recreation	7.00	.03	3905
783 Ushers, recreation	6.00	.04	3722
Protection			
I			
II			
III			
053 Foresters	10.58	1.50	5609
762 Firemen	10.50	1.26	4890
782 Sheriffs and bailiffs	—	—	—
773 Policemen and detectives	11.33	.19	5070
IV			
771 Marshals and constables	—	—	—
763 Guards	9.17	.14	4674
V			
785 Watchmen	5.50	.02	3631
Education			
I			
010 College presidents, etc.	17.20	6.40	6812
093 Teachers, n.e.c.[b]	16.40	5.00	6305
091 Sports instructors and officials	18.00	12.00	6626
II			
III			
IV			
V			
Health			
I			
032 Dentists	18.00	7.00	7617

[b] Not elsewhere classified.

Table 36. Allocation of census occupations to job families and content levels. (*continued*)

Job family and level	general education development (*years*)	specific vocational preparation (*years*)	"value of the job" based on worker traits characteristics (*dollars*)
	Estimates of:		
Health (*continued*)			
075 Physicians and surgeons	17.78	7.00	6863
071 Osteopaths	18.00	7.00	6913
098 Veterinarians	16.00	5.67	6880
070 Optometrists	16.00	3.00	6536
008 Chiropractors	16.00	3.00	6602
II			
073 Pharmacists	16.00	3.00	5479
094 Technicians, medical and dental	12.36	1.80	5193
097 Therapists, n.e.c.[b]	14.00	2.12	5865
034 Dieticians	16.00	3.00	6221
III			
058 Nurses	12.00	2.50	5127
054 Funeral directors	12.00	3.00	5127
302 Attendants, physician's or dentist's office	9.50	1.58	5040
IV			
781 Practical nurses	10.00	1.50	4798
730 Attendants, hospital	9.50	.10	4697
059 Nurses, student professional	—	—	—
772 Midwives	—	—	—
V			
Welfare			
I			
009 Clergymen	—	—	—
077 Recreation group workers	16.00	5.00	6231
079 Social workers, except group	15.50	3.92	6167
II			
078 Religious workers	—	—	—
III			
IV			
V			

[b] Not elsewhere classified.

Table 36. Allocation of census occupations to job families
and content levels. (*continued*)

Job family and level	Estimates of:		
	general education development (years)	*specific vocational preparation (years)*	*"value of the job" based on worker traits characteristics (dollars)*
Administrative and organizational			
I			
055 Lawyers and judges	18.00	6.35	6626
072 Personnel & labor relations workers	16.80	4.08	6406
036 Editors and reporters	15.67	4.65	6199
II			
099 Professional, technical and kindred workers, n.e.c.[b]	14.91	2.55	6402
052 Farm, home management advisers	14.67	2.06	5987
291 Managers, officials, n.e.c.,[b] salaried	12.50	3.54	5618
III			
292 Managers, officials, n.e.c.,[b] self-employed	11.46	5.06	5056
270 Postmasters	—	—	—
250 Officials, public administration	13.20	3.26	5746
IV			
260 Officials, lodge, society or union	11.00	.04	5343
V			
230 Managers, building	—	—	—
Research and design			
I			
033 Designers	15.60	4.90	6806
040 Engineers, technical	15.20	4.60	7437
080 Social scientists, n.e.c.[b]	17.33	3.00	7179
060 Natural scientists, n.e.c.[b]	17.20	3.18	7127
007 Chemists	11.35	3.16	6591
003 Architects	—	—	—
II			
035 Draftsmen	12.68	2.68	6642
III			
IV			
V			

[b] Not elsewhere classified.

APPENDIX II
A STATISTICAL TEST
OF THE JOB-CONTENT FRAMEWORK

The principles of the job-content model are intended to group together similar types of work, with respect to the technical focus and level of content involved. If these concepts are reflected in the present, admittedly experimental, set of families and content levels, then the types of work and the concomitant demands on workers' skills, abilities, and training should be more alike within the cells of the matrix than between them. The existence of a clear hypothesis of this nature suggests the desirability of some sort of statistical analysis to test the classification here presented. In this regard, two questions must be faced: On what variable should the test be performed? What form should the test itself take?

Choice of Variable

It has been argued that job content is one of the underlying factors relating to worker compensation in a market economy. If the job-content matrix developed in this study does reflect variations in job content, one could analyze the variations in income levels by job families and content levels. Presumably, such an analysis would show significant and corroborating results—particularly as income levels entered indirectly into the proceedings for setting up content levels. Hence, use of median occupational income levels would not appear to provide a legitimate test of the job-content model and its present application.

A better variable for testing the experimental classification exists—namely, the rate of change of income between two census dates. In the first place, this variable did not enter the procedures through which occupations were classified. Secondly, if other factors affecting wage differentials (age, sex, race, unionization, industrial and geographical distributions) change relatively slowly over time, then widely varying changes in demand for the jobs in a cell of the matrix (pool of skill) should nonetheless be associated with highly similar income changes for all jobs in the cell, as suggested in Chapter 4.

Methods and Test

It seems appealing to apply an analysis of variance to the cells of the job-content matrix, testing whether rows (content levels) and columns (job families) affect our chosen test variable. Unfortunately, a glance at Table 17 in Chapter 3 reveals the following situation: of the 90 cells in the matrix, 26 are void, and 19 have only one census occupation assigned to them. The fact that half the the cells have no variance within them makes a standard variance analysis suspect. It should also be noted that a simple comparison of the amount explained by a system with 90 classes vis-à-vis one with eight or ten tells us very little—as the number of classifications approaches the number of observations, the proportion of variance that is "between group" must approach the total.

To avoid these difficulties, the following approach was employed. Dummy variables were assigned to the rows and columns of the job-content matrix, so that each census occupation was described by a 1 denoting its column (job family) and a 1 denoting its row (content level), with zeros everywhere else. Since one row and one column must be deleted in this approach, there were thus 21 dummy variables used. In order to analyze the contributions of family effects and content-level effects separately, the regression was run in two blocks—on the family dummies, then on families and columns together. The first regression, on job family effects only, resulted in an R^2 of .1648 (significant at the 1 per cent level). When content levels were added to the regression, R^2 rose to .1802 (still significant at 1 per cent). The regressions and their coefficients need not be presented, as the only use for the coefficients is as part of the method for estimating effects of families and content levels on wage changes.

The important results of this regression analysis are summarized below, as the estimated row and column effects around the mean. (Item 8 is referred to as Sales

Family	*Deviation*
1. Tools focus—specialized	−2.0
2. Tools focus—nonspecialized	+4.5
3. Machines and equipment focus—specialized	−6.7
4. Machines and equipment focus—nonspecialized	+10.8
5. Inspection	−5.6
6. Vehicle operation	−0.2
7. Farm	−3.1
8. Sales—considerable knowledge of product required	−2.3
9. Sales—little knowledge of product required	−7.6
10. Clerical workers	+3.8
11. Personal service	−13.8
12. Entertainment	−5.3
13. Protection	+2.9
14. Education	−0.9
15. Health	+4.5
16. Welfare	+2.0
17. Administrative and organizational	+1.3
18. Research and design	+16.2

Content level	*Deviation*
I	+3.8
II	+3.6
III	−0.5
IV	−2.7
V	−4.6

Table 37. Analysis of variance.

Source	Sum of squares	d.f.	Mean square	F
Total	4.7921	206		
Job family effects	.7906	17	.0465	2.19
Content-level effects	.0739	4	.0185	.87
Unexplained	3.9326	185	.0213	—

A in all tables; item 9, as Sales B.) The unweighted mean increase in median wage and salary income from 1950 to 1960 was 63.6 per cent; the figures shown reflect the average percentage-point deviations by family and content level from that mean. It can be seen that several job families had sizable impacts on rates of income increase, notably research and design, nonspecialized machines and equipment, health, and nonspecialized tools. Several families exercised negative effects revealed in the variance analysis—particularly personal services, sales jobs requiring little product knowledge, specialized machines and equipment jobs, inspection, and entertainment. The rank order correlation-coefficient between these deviations and the 1950–1960 rates of growth shown in Table 39 of Appendix III is +0.41. Levels of content show impacts directly related to content levels, but as the subsequent analysis indicates, they were not significant.

With the regression results, a two-way analysis of variance can be performed, testing the importance of families and levels. This procedure is summarized in Table 37, where the total sum of squares to be explained is broken down into categories—(a) explained by the families, (b) explained by the content levels, and (c) unexplained variance. The first component is estimated by applying the R^2 from the family-only regression to the total sum of squares, and the second component by the additional variance explained by adding content-level dummies to the regression. Finally, an F-test can be performed on the ratios of mean squares.

As the table indicates, the F-test shows job family effects significant at the 1 per cent level, but no significant effects from content levels. This, in fact, is what we should be led to expect from the theory underlying this scheme of classification. Job families are unified by types of work, promotion patterns, and so forth, and their rates of change of wages do move together. The basic theory, however, does not contain any material which would predict that content levels would have significant and differing impacts, that is, to predict changes in skill differentials.

APPENDIX III

The three tables in this appendix contain data used in preparing the projections of Chapter 4 and some results of these projections. Table 38 shows 1970 estimated employment for major industries by region of the country, derived from the National Planning Association projections. Table 39 shows decennial growth rates for the past twenty years and the next ten years for all job families by content level. Table 40 compares the effects of changing industrial employment coefficients in employment for the two decades from 1950 to 1970.

Table 38. Employment estimates for industries by regions, adapted from NPA projections, 1970.

(thousands)

| Industry (census classification) | Northeast | | | | | |
	I	II	III	IV	V	Total
Total	2082	3550	7255	2809	5080	20776
Agriculture	2	6	18	165	93	284
Mining	6	15	24	21	0	66
Construction	49	186	775	38	231	1279
Manufacturing	404	1495	1579	392	2339	6209
Transportation	48	244	796	55	140	1283
Trade	143	495	1201	1307	839	3985
Finance	25	414	557	48	18	1062
Services	1308	609	1681	694	1376	5668
Public administration	97	86	624	89	44	940

| Industry | Northcentral | | | | | |
	I	II	III	IV	V	Total
Total	1918	3461	7150	3417	4308	20254
Agriculture	10	26	83	768	432	1319
Mining	9	23	38	33	0	103
Construction	52	199	827	41	246	1365
Manufacturing	405	1500	1584	393	1347	5229
Transportation	49	250	815	58	144	1316
Trade	153	530	1286	1400	899	4268
Finance	20	321	432	37	14	824
Services	1120	523	1443	596	1181	4863
Public administration	100	89	642	91	45	967

Table 38. Employment estimates for industries by regions, adapted from NPA projections, 1970.

(thousands)   (*continued*)

Industry	*South*					
	I	*II*	*III*	*IV*	*V*	*Total*
Total	1787	3014	6797	3493	4589	19680
Agriculture	12	31	98	910	512	1563
Mining	32	80	130	114	2	358
Construction	58	221	919	46	273	1517
Manufacturing	269	997	1052	262	1560	4140
Transportation	49	247	808	57	142	1303
Trade	152	526	1277	1390	893	4238
Finance	19	306	412	35	13	785
Services	1087	509	1400	579	1145	4720
Public administration	109	97	701	100	49	1056

Industry	*West*					
	I	*II*	*III*	*IV*	*V*	*Total*
Total	1123	1790	4897	1821	2617	12248
Agriculture	4	10	32	298	167	511
Mining	10	25	41	36	1	113
Construction	33	128	531	26	158	876
Manufacturing	157	581	613	152	908	2411
Transportation	29	147	1202	34	85	1497
Trade	87	302	733	798	512	2432
Finance	11	188	253	22	8	482
Services	700	327	901	371	736	3035
Public administration	92	82	591	84	42	891

Table 39. Decennial rates of growth by job families and job-content levels, 1940–1960, and etsimates to 1970.

(per cent)

Job family and content level	1940–1950	1950–1960	1960–1970 estimates
Tools—specialized	38.2	−6.7	−3.8
I	92.3	76.0	71.0
II	20.6	−6.4	−11.4
III	45.8	2.9	11.7
IV	19.5	−12.6	−16.1
V	56.6	−16.1	−16.5
Tools—nonspecialized	38.9	5.7	10.4
I	25.0	20.0	25.2
II	63.7	20.4	25.3
III	61.2	7.3	13.9
IV	34.7	22.8	18.8
V	11.5	−9.0	−6.3
Machines and equipment— specialized	25.3	−21.9	−1.8
I	—	—	—
II	45.5	19.4	27.1
III	121.3	14.1	23.9
IV	1.4	−47.5	−40.6
V	—	—	—
Machines and equipment— nonspecialized	38.5	10.7	5.2
I	—	—	—
II	—	—	—
III	10.9	21.9	19.8
IV	35.1	−17.3	−37.0
V	40.6	10.9	5.5
Inspection	53.8	51.4	44.9
I	—	—	—
II	57.1	57.8	47.2
III	47.9	33.5	39.5
IV	21.4	17.6	2.1
V	31.8	−24.1	−18.4
Vehicle operation	24.9	16.6	24.1
I	—	—	—
II	17.9	−10.0	−2.3
III	28.9	18.9	23.5
IV	2.0	−22.0	−19.4
V	14.2	30.1	46.8

Table 39. Decennial rates of growth by job families and job-content levels, 1940–
1960, and estimates to 1970.

(per cent)   (*continued*)

Job family and content level	1940–1950	1950–1960	1960–1970 estimates
Farm	−18.6	−41.1	−20.9
I	—	—	—
II	−5.4	−31.4	−9.5
III	−29.2	47.1	30.3
IV	−16.2	−41.9	−21.5
V	−22.6	−40.4	−20.3
Sales A	34.1	24.5	28.7
I	102.9	64.8	69.0
II	27.5	31.0	11.4
III	26.2	−4.8	11.0
IV	—	—	—
V	—	—	—
Sales B	35.6	16.9	29.2
I	—	—	—
II	—	—	—
III	58.3	31.6	52.2
IV	36.5	13.4	27.1
V	12.4	107.6	60.8
Clerical	57.8	35.6	32.9
I	68.1	28.5	43.6
II	15.4	75.6	60.8
III	54.9	34.4	30.9
IV	135.9	62.0	58.0
V	−7.4	0.0	2.5
Personal service	−1.1	23.5	39.4
I	—	—	—
II	—	—	—
III	19.6	28.7	42.9
IV	−25.9	25.0	40.3
V	−0.5	21.5	38.7
Entertainment	34.0	12.9	18.4
I	27.6	27.3	18.5
II	33.3	75.0	38.2
III	43.3	−20.9	19.9
IV	200.0	−26.7	−24.1
V	36.7	−14.6	23.2

Table 39. Decennial rates of growth by job families and job-content levels, 1940–
1960, and estimates to 1970.

(per cent)   (*continued*)

Job family and content level	*1940–1950*	*1950–1960*	*1960–1970 estimates*
Protection	30.4	19.9	10.2
I	—	—	—
II	—	—	—
III	44.0	28.5	33.3
IV	19.0	2.5	2.9
V	−25.0	108.3	84.3
Education	15.6	49.3	24.4
I	15.6	49.3	24.4
II	—	—	—
III	—	—	—
IV	—	—	—
V	—	—	—
Health	44.9	40.8	31.4
I	15.6	15.3	1.1
II	113.0	38.9	34.3
III	13.2	44.1	25.1
IV	123.5	57.0	51.2
V	—	—	—
Welfare	24.6	30.0	7.7
I	25.5	29.0	7.1
II	19.3	36.0	14.2
III	—	—	—
IV	—	—	—
V	—	—	—
Administrative and organizational	32.0	11.3	17.9
I	36.4	27.6	14.4
II	51.5	51.9	50.2
III	21.8	−18.7	−19.9
IV	8.0	22.2	−11.6
V	−4.3	−19.7	−72.2
Research and design	103.1	60.0	48.6
I	114.7	57.5	48.0
II	52.9	75.3	57.9
III	—	—	—
IV	—	—	—
V	—	—	—

Table 40. Employment effects of intra-industry coefficient changes, 1950 to 1960, and estimates to 1970.

(thousands)

Job family and content level	Employment effects due to "technical changes in industries"	
	1950–1960	1960–1970 estimates
Tools—specialized	−513	−618
I	14	19
II	−56	−60
III	−92	−115
IV	−173	−207
V	−206	−255
Tools—nonspecialized	−808	−986
I	2	2
II	141	168
III	−291	−401
IV	−44	−52
V	−616	−702
Machines and equipment— specialized	−132	−116
I	—	—
II	17	17
III	5	18
IV	−154	−151
V	—	—
Machines and equipment— nonspecialized	−421	−469
I	—	—
II	—	—
III	18	17
IV	−82	−91
V	−357	−395
Inspection	433	508
I	—	—
II	404	469
III	39	52
IV	−2	−3
V	−8	−10

Table 40. Employment effects of intra-industry coefficient changes, 1950 to 1960, and estimates to 1970.

(thousands)   (*continued*)

Job family and content level	*Employment effects due to "technical changes in industries"*	
	1950–1960	*1960–1970 estimates*
Vehicle operation	355	357
I	—	—
II	−6	−5
III	306	284
IV	−20	−19
V	75	97
Farm	−367	−199
I	—	—
II	2	2
III	14	11
IV	−313	−142
V	−70	−70
Sales A	38	50
I	74	96
II	−19	−26
III	−17	−20
IV	—	—
V	—	—
Sales B	193	204
I	—	—
II	—	—
III	16	20
IV	73	64
V	104	120
Clerical	914	1209
I	13	109
II	21	26
III	712	852
IV	182	234
V	−14	−12

Table 40. Employment effects of intra-industry coefficient changes, 1950 to 1960, and estimates to 1970.

(thousands)   (*continued*)

| Job family and content level | Employment effects due to "technical changes in industries" | |
	1950–1960	1960–1970 estimates
Personal service	345	456
I	—	—
II	—	—
III	98	131
IV	75	87
V	172	238
Entertainment	−40	−56
I	−29	−41
II	6	4
III	−6	−5
IV	−4	−6
V	−7	−8
Protection	−1	39
I	—	—
II	—	—
III	23	63
IV	−37	−41
V	13	17
Education	−155	−209
I	−155	−209
II	—	—
III	—	—
IV	—	—
V	—	—
Health	−101	−79
I	−89	−118
II	3	4
III	−50	−70
IV	35	105
V	—	—

Table 40. Employment effects of intra-industry coefficient changes, 1950 to 1960, and estimates to 1970.

	(thousands)	(continued)
	Employment effects due to "technical changes in industries"	
Job family and content level	1950–1960	1960–1970 estimates
Welfare	−74	−98
I	−65	−86
II	−9	−12
III	—	—
IV	—	—
V	—	—
Administrative and organizational	−177	−286
I	−24	−40
II	696	825
III	−797	−1006
IV	−12	−16
V	−40	−49
Research and design	347	411
I	279	331
II	68	80
III	—	—
IV	—	—
V	—	—

APPENDIX IV

This appendix presents the detailed job-content estimates.

Table 41. Job content by sex (male), 1940, 1950 and 1960 (Part I).
(thousands)

	Tools		Mach. & equip.		Inspection	Vehicle operation	Farm	Clerical	Sales A	Sales B
	spec.	nonspec.	spec.	nonspec.						
Total	1477	6147	962	3134	666	2114	7762	2059	700	1800
	1969	8415	1080	4273	1023	2602	6119	2640	897	2168
	1872	8996	860	4728	1589	3050	3587	3156	1090	2474
I	13	7	0	0	0	0	0	137	52	0
	24	8	0	0	0	0	0	326	107	0
	43	9	0	0	0	0	0	404	182	0
II	238	1152	94	0	528	152	36	28	409	0
	279	1881	131	0	832	176	34	30	495	0
	263	2281	162	0	1346	162	23	43	637	0
III	577	2051	149	312	115	1577	24	1645	239	23
	807	3216	293	346	164	2006	16	1990	295	32
	846	3515	354	417	217	2388	24	2329	272	30
IV	353	387	719	153	14	106	4956	179	0	1675
	432	514	656	206	16	107	4140	242	0	2016
	390	626	344	172	19	85	2374	326	0	2238
V	296	2549	0	2669	9	278	2746	66	0	102
	426	2795	0	3720	11	313	1929	52	0	119
	331	2566	0	4139	7	414	1165	53	0	206

[a] In each triplet of figures, the top number refers to 1940. One reads down to 1950 and 1960.

	Personal services	Enter-tainment	Protection	Admin. & org.	Research & design	Education	Health	Welfare	Total
Total	1381	186	457	3367	412	320	449	167	33560
	1451	238	579	4227	795	415	531	202	39623
	1502	248	692	4751	1311	663	665	273	41506
I	0	104	0	217	334	320	260	158	1606
	0	123	0	263	686	415	274	190	2415
	0	148	0	334	1110	663	346	251	3491
II	0	8	0	1144	78	0	86	9	3964
	0	10	0	1637	109	0	123	12	5748
	0	20	0	2467	201	0	156	22	7782
III	386	16	239	1944	0	0	45	0	9343
	410	23	332	2258	0	0	47	0	12237
	439	14	437	1887	0	0	51	0	13218
IV	243	4	202	21	0	0	58	0	9072
	270	10	235	25	0	0	87	0	8957
	315	8	242	30	0	0	112	0	7281
V	751	53	16	40	0	0	0	0	9575
	771	72	12	43	0	0	0	0	10275
	749	58	14	33	0	0	0	0	9375

Table 41. Job content by sex (female), 1940, 1950 and 1960 (Part II).
(thousands)

	Tools		Mach. & equip.		Inspection	Vehicle operation	Farm	Clerical	Sales A	Sales B
	spec.	nonspec.	spec.	nonspec.						
Total	360	157	18	1685	77	13	472	2375	59	764
	570	342	148	2402	120	55	587	4355	120	1314
	498	360	100	2558	223	47	363	6340	176	1595
I	0	1	0	0	0	0	0	120	18	0
	2	2	0	0	0	0	0	105	35	0
	1	2	0	0	0	0	0	151	52	0
II	10	19	6	0	57	0	1	11	32	0
	20	37	13	0	87	5	1	15	67	0
	17	29	10	0	104	0	1	36	98	0
III	22	1	11	1	6	8	0	2240	9	14
	68	90	61	1	15	39	0	4032	18	25
	54	34	50	7	23	43	1	5767	26	45
IV	159	39	2	1	0	0	151	5	0	747
	179	60	75	2	1	2	141	192	0	1290
	145	79	40	1	1	0	112	376	0	1512
V	170	96	0	1683	13	4	320	3	0	3
	301	153	0	2399	17	9	445	11	0	0
	280	116	0	2651	15	5	249	11	0	39

[a] In each triplet of figures, the top number refers to 1940. One reads down to 1950 and 1960.

106

	Personal services	Entertainment	Protection	Education	Health	Welfare	Admin. & org.	Research & design	Total
Total	3056	102	4	796	532	74	452	12	11007
	2935	148	23	876	890	98	812	65	15852
	3913	189	30	1263	1335	117	856	65	19950
I	0	77	0	796	12	48	19	10	1097
	0	108	0	876	39	69	59	53	1347
	0	146	0	1263	15	83	77	53	1843
II	0	4	0	0	13	26	119	1	298
	0	6	0	0	38	29	277	12	657
	0	8	0	0	137	34	439	12	926
III	385	14	2	0	378	0	282	0	3375
	513	20	14	0	432	0	453	0	5780
	749	20	9	0	639	0	317	0	7785
IV	482	1	2	0	128	0	4	0	1722
	268	4	9	0	331	0	1	0	2556
	356	3	9	0	544	0	3	0	3180
V	2189	6	0	0	0	0	28	0	4515
	2155	11	0	0	0	0	22	0	5512
	2808	12	12	0	0	0	30	0	6216

Table 42. Job content by regions, 1940, 1950 and 1960. (thousands)[a]

Northeastern

	Tools		Mach. & equip.		Inspection	Vehicle operation	Farm	Sales A	Sales B
	spec.	nonspec.	spec.	nonspec.					
Total	631	1930	305	2031	242	623	576	262	828
	739	2379	350	2539	359	699	481	321	982
	630	2323	210	2487	500	734	297	360	1104
I	3	4	—	—	—	—	—	23	—
	5	5	—	—	—	—	—	44	—
	8	5	—	—	—	—	—	69	—
II	101	408	32	—	201	44	7	144	—
	112	596	44	—	300	51	6	159	—
	95	670	50	—	434	39	3	187	—
III	212	627	66	93	38	498	3	94	12
	269	874	122	107	55	554	2	117	16
	257	867	102	120	63	606	1	105	18
IV	168	119	207	55	0	4	325	—	786
	169	132	184	70	1	23	274	—	943
	126	144	58	53	1	13	169	—	1032
V	147	771	—	1883	1	77	242	—	30
	183	772	—	2361	2	72	200	—	23
	145	638	—	2314	2	77	124	—	55

[a] In each triplet of figures, the top number refers to 1940. One reads down to 1950 and 1960.

Northeastern

	Clerical	Personal services	Enter- tainment	Protection	Admin. & org.	Research & design	Education	Health	Welfare	Total
Total	1614	1311	97	178	1160	164	306	338	76	12671
	2264	1184	121	208	1493	294	327	451	81	15280
	2825	1285	128	229	1475	417	471	578	102	16157
I	82	—	65	—	84	132	306	90	62	545
	141	—	78	—	109	249	327	103	68	801
	164	—	86	—	132	349	471	111	83	1006
II	12	—	5	—	400	32	—	32	14	1738
	12	—	7	—	562	44	—	67	12	2301
	21	—	11	—	806	68	—	83	19	2957
III	1437	233	10	99	638	—	—	152	—	4212
	1975	250	13	120	784	—	—	158	—	5418
	2439	284	11	140	507	—	—	200	—	5719
IV	52	135	1	74	8	—	—	64	—	1999
	111	180	4	84	8	—	—	123	—	2313
	174	158	3	79	9	—	—	184	—	2203
V	31	942	16	6	31	—	—	—	—	4177
	25	754	19	5	30	—	—	—	—	4448
	27	843	17	10	21	—	—	—	—	4273

Table 42. Job content by regions, 1940, 1950 and 1960.
(thousands)

Northcentral states

	Tools		Mach. & equip.		Inspection	Vehicle operation	Farm	Sales A	Sales B
	spec.	nonspec.	spec.	nonspec.					
Total	497	2065	200	1431	230	674	2647	247	320
	671	2761	217	2190	362	804	2330	318	1078
	608	2833	197	2297	503	885	1504	362	1206
I	3	2	—	—	—	—	—	23	—
	5	3	—	—	—	—	—	45	—
	9	3	—	—	—	—	—	68	—
II	75	461	31	—	192	49	10	138	—
	87	656	44	—	307	56	10	167	—
	78	780	50	—	432	46	5	203	—
III	180	657	50	105	35	489	3	86	12
	258	1008	75	123	51	603	2	106	18
	250	1044	94	139	68	682	2	91	23
IV	162	158	119	54	2	19	1820	—	775
	183	206	98	81	2	42	1633	—	1019
	151	230	53	69	2	30	1129	—	1099
V	77	787	—	1272	0	116	814	—	33
	138	887	—	1987	2	102	686	—	41
	120	776	—	2090	1	127	368	—	85

(continued)

Northcentral states

	Clerical	Personal services	Enter-tainment	Protection	Admin. & org.	Research & design	Education	Health	Welfare	Total
Total	1404	1156	85	154	1183	132	356	297	75	13632
	2173	1142	112	166	1446	259	381	417	91	16866
	2750	1407	119	187	1503	380	554	586	113	17994
I	77	—	56	—	69	103	356	90	64	488
	131	—	68	—	91	218	381	95	78	733
	158	—	86	—	109	310	554	103	96	943
II	13	—	2	—	402	28	—	30	10	1796
	14	—	2	—	581	41	—	61	13	2371
	23	—	5	—	800	69	—	80	16	3143
III	1232	235	6	69	694	—	—	127	—	3983
	1873	264	9	90	756	—	—	137	—	5372
	2340	341	6	110	577	—	—	194	—	5960
IV	64	89	1	59	8	—	—	51	—	3380
	138	125	4	72	8	—	—	125	—	3736
	213	116	2	70	10	—	—	208	—	3382
V	18	832	19	5	11	—	—	—	—	3985
	17	752	29	4	10	—	—	—	—	4655
	16	950	20	7	7	—	—	—	—	4566

Table 42. Job content by regions, 1940, 1950 and 1960.
(thousands)

South

	Tools		Mach. & equip.		Inspection	Vehicle operation	Farm	Sales A	Sales B
	spec.	nonspec.	spec.	nonspec.					
Total	472	1646	345	1061	177	589	4296	160	604
	770	2390	525	1451	276	808	3184	232	940
	745	2629	403	1828	439	1013	1607	323	1125
I	4	1	—	—	—	—	—	13	—
	9	2	—	—	—	—	—	31	—
	16	2	—	—	—	—	—	56	—
II	48	184	21	—	131	39	14	100	—
	69	339	34	—	213	47	14	140	—
	71	505	42	—	359	48	12	199	—
III	136	514	26	76	31	444	10	48	7
	229	964	114	77	45	633	7	62	14
	250	1047	145	104	65	795	11	68	20
IV	122	93	298	34	6	26	2570	—	570
	176	146	377	41	8	29	2000	—	893
	166	196	216	34	8	27	931	—	1044
V	162	853	—	951	8	81	1702	—	27
	287	940	—	1332	10	99	1162	—	32
	243	879	—	1690	8	143	653	—	61

(continued)

112

South

	Clerical	Personal services	Entertainment	Protection	Admin. & org.	Research & design	Education	Health	Welfare	Total
Total	915	1513	54	101	957	75	330	217	65	13575
	1616	1489	79	142	1334	180	406	339	87	16251
	2343	1896	95	189	1616	299	579	508	114	17751
I	55	—	31	—	56	63	330	58	58	340
	90	—	45	—	79	159	406	69	79	562
	131	—	66	—	105	259	579	84	102	821
II	8	—	2	—	298	12	—	22	6	1214
	12	—	2	—	501	22	—	51	8	1856
	21	—	4	—	781	40	—	74	12	2745
III	790	195	5	45	591	—	—	89	—	3007
	1378	272	10	80	739	—	—	108	—	4733
	1976	368	7	115	713	—	—	175	—	5859
IV	49	183	10	51	4	—	—	48	—	4056
	124	144	4	64	6	—	—	110	—	4120
	204	157	3	67	7	—	—	175	—	3236
V	14	1135	14	4	7	—	—	—	—	4958
	14	1073	18	2	10	—	—	—	—	4980
	12	1371	15	6	9	—	—	—	—	5090

Table 42. Job content by regions, 1940, 1950 and 1960.
(thousands)

West

	Tools		Mach. & equip.		Inspection	Vehicle operation	Farm	Sales A	Sales B
	spec.	*nonspec.*	*spec.*	*nonspec.*					
Total	237	662	130	296	95	242	714	90	312
	360	1158	137	495	146	345	710	146	482
	387	1470	149	773	290	465	542	221	634
I	3	0	—	—	—	—	—	10	—
	6	0	—	—	—	—	—	22	—
	11	1	—	—	—	—	—	20	—
II	23	114	15	—	61	21	6	60	—
	32	222	22	—	98	27	5	96	—
	36	356	29	—	226	29	5	168	—
III	72	258	18	38	17	167	8	20	5
	119	496	42	40	28	254	6	27	8
	144	590	64	61	44	349	10	34	14
IV	60	56	98	11	5	14	392	—	292
	84	90	73	16	7	15	373	—	452
	93	135	56	17	9	14	258	—	575
V	79	234	—	247	12	38	308	—	15
	119	349	—	440	14	50	325	—	22
	104	390	—	696	10	72	270	—	45

(continued)

West	Clerical	Personal services	Enter-tainment	Protection	Admin. & org.	Research & design	Education	Health	Welfare	Total
Total	502	457	51	49	517	53	125	129	26	4687
	947	571	74	84	766	128	176	214	41	6980
	1581	827	94	117	1004	280	322	329	62	9548
I	33	—	28	—	27	45	125	35	22	204
	70	—	40	—	43	112	176	46	34	375
	102	—	56	—	65	245	322	63	53	615
II	6	—	4	—	163	8	—	16	4	625
	8	—	4	—	270	15	—	33	8	1014
	14	—	8	—	510	36	—	56	8	1802
III	436	108	8	27	302	—	—	55	—	1541
	801	136	11	55	431	—	—	76	—	2533
	1346	194	10	80	406	—	—	122	—	3468
IV	20	101	0	21	4	—	—	24	—	1098
	61	88	3	27	5	—	—	60	—	1354
	111	95	3	34	7	—	—	88	—	1494
V	6	248	10	1	20	—	—	—	—	1218
	7	346	16	1	16	—	—	—	—	1704
	9	538	18	2	16	—	—	—	—	2169

Table 43. Job content by major census industry, 1950 and 1960.
(thousands)ᵃ

Agriculture, forestry and fisheries

	Tools spec.	Tools nonspec.	Mach. & equip. spec.	Mach. & equip. nonspec.	Inspection	Vehicle operation	Farm	Sales A	Sales B
Total	4 / 2	47 / 49	69 / 36	23 / 37	6 / 13	34 / 69	6701 / 3948	2 / 0	5 / 10
I	0 / 0	— / —	— / —	— / —	— / —	— / —	— / —	— / —	— / —
II	1 / 0	6 / 10	0 / —	— / —	4 / 6	1 / 3	36 / 24	1 / 0	— / —
III	1 / 0	7 / 8	2 / 2	1 / 0	0 / 5	31 / 66	17 / 24	0 / 0	0 / 0
IV	0 / 0	0 / 0	67 / 34	1 / 0	0 / 0	2 / 0	4258 / 2490	— / —	4 / 9
V	1 / 0	34 / 30	— / —	21 / 35	0 / 1	0 / —	2390 / 1410	— / —	0 / 0

Agriculture, forestry and fisheries

	Clerical	Personal services	Enter-tainment	Protection	Admin. & org.	Research & design	Education	Health	Welfare	Total
Total	18 / 32	40 / 69	0 / 0	17 / 20	26 / 30	5 / 4	3 / 4	11 / 17	0 / 0	7013 / 4340
I	0 / 1	— / —	0 / 0	— / —	— / 0	5 / 4	3 / 4	9 / 13	0 / 0	19 / 22
II	0 / —	— / —	0 / 0	— / —	13 / 18	0 / 0	— / —	0 / 0	— / —	64 / 62
III	18 / 30	3 / 3	— / 0	15 / 18	12 / 12	— / —	— / —	0 / 0	— / —	109 / 171
IV	0 / —	36 / 63	0 / 0	2 / 2	— / —	— / —	— / —	2 / 4	— / —	4373 / 2605
V	0 / 0	2 / 2	— / —	— / —	0 / —	— / —	— / —	— / —	— / —	2449 / 1479

ᵃ The top figure in each pair of numbers refers to 1950.

Mining

	Tools		Mach. & equip.		Inspection	Vehicle operation	Farm	Sales A	Sales B
	spec.	nonspec.	spec.	nonspec.					
Total	20	68	578	42	45	59	—	2	2
	12	65	308	37	44	47	—	2	3
I	2	—	—	—	—	—	—	—	—
	1	—	—	—	—	—	—	—	—
II	0	29	0	—	38	1	—	1	—
	0	33	0	—	40	2	—	1	—
III	16	31	14	39	7	57	—	0	0
	9	25	17	35	3	45	—	0	0
IV	2	8	363	2	—	0	—	—	2
	2	7	291	1	—	0	—	—	3
V	0	—	—	—	—	0	—	—	—
	0	—	—	—	—	0	—	—	—

Mining

	Clerical	Personal services	Entertainment	Protection	Admin. & org.	Research & design	Education	Health	Welfare	Total
Total	46	1	0	5	38	21	0	0	0	927
	54	2	—	5	39	31	0	0	0	647
I	4	—	—	—	1	20	0	0	0	28
	7	—	—	—	2	28	0	0	0	38
II	0	—	—	—	18	1	—	—	—	89
	0	—	—	—	24	3	—	—	—	103
III	41	0	—	5	18	—	—	0	—	225
	47	0	—	5	14	—	—	0	—	197
IV	—	0	0	4	—	—	—	—	—	583
	—	0	—	3	—	—	—	—	—	306
V	0	0	—	0	0	—	—	—	—	2
	0	0	—	—	—	—	—	—	—	2

Table 43. Job content by major census industry, 1950 and 1960.
(thousands)

Construction

	Tools		Mach. & equip.		Inspection	Vehicle operation	Farm	Sales A	Sales B
	spec.	nonspec.	spec.	nonspec.					
Total	346	2158	77	85	67	117	—	6	11
	356	2155	153	114	120	161	—	5	15
I	6	0	—	—	—	—	—	—	—
	14	0	—	—	—	—	—	—	—
II	2	104	1	—	59	1	—	4	—
	0	140	0	—	102	2	—	4	—
III	252	1398	75	19	8	115	—	1	2
	260	1360	152	21	17	158	—	0	2
IV	84	10	0	2	0	0	—	—	9
	80	14	—	2	0	0	—	—	14
V	0	646	—	64	—	0	—	—	0
	0	641	—	91	—	0	—	—	—

Construction

	Clerical	Personal services	Entertainment	Protection	Admin. & org.	Research & design	Education	Health	Welfare	Total
Total	117	6	0	8	293	95	0	0	0	3386
	168	14	0	7	399	112	0	0	—	3781
I	9	—	0	—	1	83	0	0	0	101
	12	—	0	—	2	99	0	0	—	128
II	0	—	—	—	98	12	—	0	—	232
	0	—	0	—	169	13	—	—	—	432
III	106	1	0	1	194	—	—	0	—	2172
	155	6	—	1	227	—	—	0	—	2360
IV	0	2	—	6	—	—	—	0	—	115
	0	4	—	6	—	—	—	0	—	121
V	0	2	—	0	0	—	—	—	—	716
	0	4	—	0	0	—	—	—	—	740

Manufacturing—durable goods

	Tools		Mach. & equip.		Inspection	Vehicle operation	Farm	Sales A	Sales B
	spec.	nonspec.	spec.	nonspec.					
Total	416	2299	18	1644	340	162	—	115	114
	375	2536	25	1208	604	225	—	136	164
I	0	2	—	—	—	—	—	—	—
	0	4	—	—	—	—	—	—	—
II	16	887	3	—	309	4	—	23	—
	17	1081	6	—	574	6	—	43	—
III	43	648	14	137	17	140	—	92	2
	46	800	18	186	15	196	—	93	2
IV	188	80	0	117	14	15	—	—	111
	193	84	0	110	16	18	—	—	163
V	169	682	—	2390	—	3	—	—	0
	118	568	—	1895	—	3	—	—	0

Manufacturing—durable goods

	Clerical	Personal services	Entertainment	Protection	Admin. & org.	Research & design	Education	Health	Welfare	Total
Total	804	36	7	62	334	264	2	10	0	7628
	1169	41	21	68	495	563	2	13	0	9645
I	55	—	6	—	15	210	2	1	0	292
	79	—	13	—	30	451	2	0	0	580
II	3	—	0	—	203	55	—	1	—	1505
	4	—	8	—	377	112	—	3	—	2230
III	738	6	0	7	116	—	—	6	—	1965
	1078	6	—	7	88	—	—	9	—	2546
IV	4	7	0	56	—	—	—	1	—	593
	4	9	0	60	—	—	—	0	—	658
V	5	23	0	—		—	—	—	—	3273
	4	26	0	—	0	—	—	—	—	3631

Table 43. Job content by major census industry, 1950 and 1960.
(thousands)

Manufacturing—nondurable goods

	Tools		Mach. & equip.		Inspection	Vehicle operation	Farm	Sales A	Sales B
	spec.	nonspec.	spec.	nonspec.					
Total	350	780	306	3030	254	190	—	120	287
	317	778	278	3183	380	354	—	126	481
I	0	4	—	—	—	—	—	—	—
	0	6	—	—	—	—	—	—	—
II	220	219	50	—	250	1	—	29	—
	217	286	80	—	362	2	—	34	—
III	45	113	167	46	3	186	—	92	2
	36	96	140	52	16	350	—	91	4
IV	56	50	88	32	0	2	—	—	191
	42	55	58	22	1	1	—	—	302
V	29	393	—	2952	—	0	—	—	93
	22	336	—	2092	—	0	—	—	175

Manufacturing—nondurable goods

	Clerical	Personal services	Enter-tainment	Protection	Admin. & org.	Research & design	Education	Health	Welfare	Total
Total	675	52	13	41	410	119	2	6	1	6637
	857	58	17	34	513	150	0	7	0	7533
I	42	—	11	—	67	112	2	0	1	240
	50	—	14	—	81	139	0	0	0	292
II	5	—	2	—	226	7	—	1	0	1012
	6	—	2	—	351	11	—	2	0	1353
III	612	6	0	3	116	—	—	3	0	1395
	782	7	0	3	82	—	—	4	0	1664
IV	8	11	0	38	—	—	—	0	—	478
	8	12	0	31	—	—	—	0	—	533
V	9	36	0	—	0	—	—	—	—	3512
	10	39	0	—	0	—	—	—	—	3690

(continued)

Transportation

	Tools		Mach. & equip.		Inspection	Vehicle operation	Farm	Sales A	Sales B
	spec.	nonspec.	spec.	nonspec.					
Total	120	666	10	154	116	1099	—	13	9
	97	495	8	111	99	1150	—	10	19
I	0	—	—	—	—	—	—	—	—
	1	—	—	—	—	—	—	—	—
II	0	81	5	—	76	159	—	4	—
	0	64	5	—	63	141	—	3	—
III	16	191	4	17	40	770	—	9	0
	10	188	3	13	36	880	—	8	0
IV	14	22	1	10	0	86	—	—	9
	8	16	0	4	0	62	—	—	19
V	89	372	—	127	0	84	—	—	0
	78	227	—	93	0	67	—	—	0

Transportation

	Clerical	Personal services	Entertainment	Protection	Admin. & org.	Research & design	Education	Health	Welfare	Total
Total	448	75	0	35	150	17	1	2	0	2920
	451	63	0	22	163	15	0	1	0	2707
I	18	—	0	—	4	15	1	0	0	39
	17	—	0	—	4	13	0	0	0	36
II	0	—	—	—	95	2	—	0	—	424
	0	—	0	—	121	2	—	0	—	400
III	410	23	—	5	52	—	—	0	—	1537
	414	24	0	6	38	—	—	0	—	1620
IV	15	6	—	21	—	—	—	0	—	186
	15	8	—	10	—	—	—	0	—	143
V	5	46	0	10	0	—	—	—	—	733
	4	32	0	6	0	—	—	—	—	508

Table 43. Job content by major census industry, 1950 and 1960.
(thousands)

Communications

| | *Tools* | | *Mach. & equip.* | | | *Vehicle* | | | |
	spec.	*nonspec.*	*spec.*	*nonspec.*	*Inspection*	*operation*	*Farm*	*Sales A*	*Sales B*
Total	135	17	0	6	12	4	—	1	1
	180	19	3	6	24	4	—	6	8
I	0	—	—	—	—	—	—	—	—
	—	—	—	—	—	—	—	—	—
II	0	5	0	—	10	0	—	0	—
	0	5	3	—	20	0	—	5	—
III	133	3	—	1	2	4	—	0	—
	179	4	—	2	4	3	—	0	—
IV	1	4	—	0	—	0	—	—	1
	0	6	—	0	—	0	—	—	8
V	0	4	—	5	0	—	—	—	—
	—	4	—	3	—	0	—	—	—

Communications

	Clerical	*Personal services*	*Entertainment*	*Protection*	*Admin. & org.*	*Research & design*	*Education*	*Health*	*Welfare*	*Total*
Total	405	6	0	0	30	18	0	0	0	638
	422	8	6	0	87	37	0	0	0	810
I	6	—	0	—	2	17	0	0	0	26
	7	—	2	—	7	34	0	0	0	50
II	0	—	—	—	27	2	—	0	—	45
	0	—	1	—	78	3	—	—	—	116
III	386	2	—	0	1	—	—	0	—	532
	405	2	0	0	2	—	—	0	—	603
IV	4	1	—	0	—	—	—	0	—	14
	5	2	2	0	—	—	—	0	—	24
V	9	3	—	—	0	—	—	—	—	22
	5	4	—	—	0	—	—	—	—	17

Utilities

	Tools spec.	Tools nonspec.	Mach. & equip. spec.	Mach. & equip. nonspec.	Inspection	Vehicle operation	Farm	Sales A	Sales B
Total	71 / 78	249 / 265	20 / 25	87 / 90	41 / 62	37 / 56	— / —	2 / 2	8 / 9
I	1 / 2	— / —	— / —	— / —	— / —	— / —	— / —	— / —	— / —
II	0 / 0	66 / 92	0 / 0	— / —	34 / 52	0 / 0	— / —	2 / 2	— / —
III	64 / 72	52 / 42	19 / 24	28 / 36	7 / 10	36 / 55	— / —	— / —	0 / 0
IV	5 / 3	11 / 12	— / —	11 / 9	— / —	0 / 0	— / —	— / —	7 / 8
V	0 / 0	120 / 119	0 / —	49 / 46	0 / —	0 / 0	— / —	— / —	0 / —

Utilities

	Clerical	Personal services	Entertainment	Protection	Admin. & org.	Research & design	Education	Health	Welfare	Total
Total	164 / 189	5 / 6	0 / 0	4 / 4	42 / 53	38 / 43	0 / 0	0 / 0	0 / —	772 / 882
I	12 / 12	— / —	0 / 0	— / —	2 / 3	33 / 35	0 / 0	0 / 0	0 / —	49 / 53
II	0 / 0	— / —	0 / —	— / —	36 / 47	5 / 8	— / —	0 / 0	— / —	146 / 203
III	141 / 166	0 / 0	— / —	3 / 4	4 / 3	— / —	— / —	0 / 0	— / —	353 / 410
IV	10 / 10	2 / 2	0 / —	— / —	— / —	— / —	— / —	0 / —	— / —	51 / 48
V	0 / 0	3 / 3	— / —	— / —	0 / 0	— / —	— / —	— / —	— / —	173 / 169

Table 43. Job content by major census industry, 1950 and 1960.

(thousands)

Trade—retail and wholesale

	Tools		Mach. & equip.		Inspection	Vehicle operation	Farm	Sales A	Sales B
	spec.	nonspec.	spec.	nonspec.					
Total	360	756	50	299	106	733	—	277	2888
	324	1099	29	330	136	827	—	349	3230
I	0	1	—	—	—	—	—	142	—
	0	0	—	—	—	—	—	233	—
II	26	154	2	—	70	3	—	30	—
	20	222	2	—	102	0	—	27	—
III	193	225	47	13	9	516	—	106	38
	196	389	27	15	11	504	—	89	60
IV	136	48	0	5	2	1	—	—	2822
	103	57	0	2	2	1	—	—	3100
V	5	328	—	281	26	213	—	—	28
	4	431	—	313	21	322	—	—	68

Trade—retail and wholesale

	Clerical	Personal services	Enter-tainment	Protection	Admin. & org.	Research & design	Education	Health	Welfare	Total
Total	1182	1360	19	19	2193	32	4	91	0	10369
	1613	1572	16	14	1971	43	5	91	0	11651
I	49	—	14	—	8	29	4	8	0	255
	44	—	14	—	11	39	5	4	0	350
II	20	—	0	—	656	3	—	80	—	1043
	25	—	0	—	820	4	—	85	—	1309
III	965	290	1	2	1530	—	—	1	—	3935
	1188	345	0	2	1139	—	—	1	—	3967
IV	139	100	2	17	—	—	—	1	—	3275
	349	119	1	12	—	—	—	0	—	3750
V	9	970	1	0	0	—	—	—	—	1862
	7	1180	0	0	0	—	—	—	—	2275

(continued)

124

Finance, insurance, and real estate

	Tools		Mach. & equip.		Inspection	Vehicle operation	Farm	Sales A	Sales B
	spec.	nonspec.	spec.	nonspec.					
Total	5	110	1	14	5	3	—	436	12
	4	112	0	12	8	5	—	592	15
I	0	—	—	—	—	—	—	—	—
	0	—	—	—	—	—	—	—	—
II	2	20	0	—	3	0	—	435	—
	2	20	0	—	4	0	—	591	—
III	1	10	0	5	2	2	—	0	0
	0	14	0	5	4	3	—	1	0
IV	1	65	0	3	—	0	—	—	11
	0	61	—	2	—	—	—	—	14
V	0	16	—	6	—	—	—	—	0
	0	16	—	6	—	0	—	—	0

Finance, insurance, and real estate

	Clerical	Personal services	Entertainment	Protection	Admin. & org.	Research & design	Education	Health	Welfare	Total
Total	823	109	0	5	327	11	0	3	0	1875
	1297	98	0	4	487	15	0	2	0	2666
I	32	—	0	—	10	10	0	0	0	53
	41	—	0	—	13	14	0	0	0	73
II	3	—	—	—	188	0	—	0	—	653
	8	—	0	—	356	1	—	0	—	984
III	756	5	0	2	67	—	—	1	—	854
	1198	5	—	0	71	—	—	0	—	1305
IV	24	53	0	13	—	—	—	1	—	171
	41	48	—	13	—	—	—	0	—	180
V	8	51	0	—	62	—	—	—	—	144
	9	45	0	—	47	—	—	—	—	125

Table 43. Job content by major census industry, 1950 and 1960.

(thousands)

Business and repair services

| | *Tools* | | *Mach. & equip.* | | | *Vehicle* | | | |
	spec.	*nonspec.*	*spec.*	*nonspec.*	*Inspection*	*operation*	*Farm*	*Sales A*	*Sales B*
Total	64	672	2	51	18	31	—	17	32
	61	636	3	78	39	47	—	18	48
I	0	0	—	—	—	—	—	—	—
	0	0	—	—	—	—	—	—	—
II	21	91	1	—	15	0	—	15	—
	17	126	3	—	34	0	—	14	—
III	23	506	0	1	2	12	—	2	6
	19	413	0	5	6	24	—	2	7
IV	20	30	0	0	0	—	—	—	26
	23	42	0	0	0	—	—	—	41
V	0	45	—	49	—	18	—	—	0
	0	54	—	72	—	23	—	—	0

Business and repair services

	Clerical	*Personal services*	*Entertainment*	*Protection*	*Admin. & org.*	*Research & design*	*Education*	*Health*	*Welfare*	*Total*
Total	246	18	12	14	193	20	2	2	0	1393
	298	40	16	31	219	54	2	3	0	1592
I	81	—	12	—	11	17	2	0	0	124
	12	—	14	—	16	44	2	0	0	90
II	0	—	0	—	59	3	2	0	0	207
	1	—	2	—	108	9	—	0	—	314
III	154	0	0	6	123	—	—	0	—	838
	269	1	0	7	96	—	—	2	—	851
IV	5	2	0	8	—	—	—	0	—	91
	9	4	—	23	—	—	—	1	—	145
V	4	15	0	—	0	—	—	—	—	133
	7	34	0	—	0	—	—	—	—	192

(continued)

Personal services

	Tools		Mach. & equip.		Inspection	Vehicle operation	Farm	Sales A	Sales B
	spec.	nonspec.	spec.	nonspec.					
Total	525 / 440	120 / 124	36 / 28	30 / 24	11 / 11	87 / 78	— / —	4 / 3	25 / 22
I	— / 0	0 / —	— / —	— / —	— / —	— / —	— / —	— / —	— / —
II	2 / 0	15 / 23	35 / 27	— / —	10 / 10	1 / 0	— / —	2 / 1	— / —
III	62 / 46	13 / 16	2 / 2	8 / 6	0 / 0	85 / 76	— / —	2 / 2	0 / 0
IV	70 / 58	19 / 17	— / —	3 / 1	— / —	0 / 0	— / —	— / —	24 / 21
V	390 / 336	73 / 68	— / —	19 / 16	0 / —	0 / 1	— / —	— / —	0 / —

Personal services

	Clerical	Personal services	Enter-tainment	Protection	Admin. & org.	Research & design	Education	Health	Welfare	Total
Total	138 / 179	2191 / 2594	6 / 9	7 / 4	203 / 211	2 / 2	1 / 2	124 / 96	2 / 3	3512 / 3831
I	5 / 5	— / —	5 / 5	— / —	1 / 0	2 / 1	1 / 2	0 / —	2 / 3	17 / 18
II	0 / 0	— / —	— / —	— / —	62 / 79	0 / 0	— / —	5 / 5	0 / —	132 / 147
III	121 / 161	426 / 517	0 / 0	3 / 1	139 / 131	— / —	— / —	45 / 40	— / —	908 / 999
IV	10 / 12	96 / 99	0 / 0	4 / 3	— / —	— / —	— / —	73 / 51	— / —	300 / 263
V	0 / 1	1670 / 1978	0 / 3	0	0 / 0	— / —	— / —	— / —	— / —	2155 / 2404

Table 43. Job content by major census industry, 1950 and 1960.
(thousands)

Entertainment and recreation services

	Tools		Mach. & equip.		Inspection	Vehicle operation	Farm	Sales A	Sales B
	spec.	nonspec.	spec.	nonspec.					
Total	7	48	29	10	7	3	—	3	13
	5	54	18	8	3	3	—	1	12
I	—	—	—	—	—	—	—	—	—
	—	—	—	—	—	—	—	—	—
II	0	10	29	—	2	0	—	2	—
	0	13	18	—	2	0	—	0	—
III	5	7	0	2	5	2	—	0	0
	4	9	0	0	2	2	—	0	0
IV	2	15	0	0	0	0	—	—	12
	0	17	0	0	0	—	—	—	12
V	0	16	—	9	—	0	—	—	1
	0	15	—	7	—	0	—	—	0

Entertainment and recreation services

	Clerical	Personal services	Enter-tainment	Protection	Admin. & org.	Research & design	Education	Health	Welfare	Total
Total	77	48	168	5	112	11	7	0	5	554
	67	84	124	6	80	1	12	0	11	491
I	3	—	44	—	6	11	7	0	5	76
	2	—	29	—	3	1	12	0	11	59
II	—	—	2	—	65	0	—	0	0	111
	0	—	0	—	48	0	—	0	—	83
III	47	8	31	0	41	—	—	0	—	150
	39	13	26	1	29	—	—	0	—	128
IV	26	14	11	4	—	—	—	0	—	84
	25	22	6	5	—	—	—	0	—	87
V	0	26	80	—	0	—	—	—	—	133
	0	48	62	—	0	—	—	—	—	134

(continued)

Professional services

	Tools spec.	Tools nonspec.	Mach. & equip. spec.	Mach. & equip. nonspec.	Inspection	Vehicle operation	Farm	Sales A	Sales B
Total	53	281	6	53	18	24	—	5	9
	82	446	12	67	51	23	—	8	16
I	6	0	—	—	—	—	—	—	—
	15	0	—	—	—	—	—	—	—
II	2	43	3	—	10	0	—	3	—
	3	85	5	—	25	1	—	6	—
III	6	37	3	17	8	22	—	1	0
	10	52	7	25	25	20	—	2	0
IV	14	169	0	12	0	0	—	—	8
	13	275	0	13	—	0	—	—	16
V	24	31	—	23	—	0	—	—	0
	41	34	—	30	—	1	—	—	0

Professional services

	Clerical	Personal services	Enter-tainment	Protection	Admin. & org.	Research & design	Education	Health	Welfare	Total
Total	651	392	155	7	295	90	1258	1123	244	4367
	1235	696	217	2	502	182	1877	1765	313	7513
I	65	—	138	—	142	77	1258	264	204	2155
	196	—	197	—	178	147	1877	342	257	3209
II	11	—	10	—	106	13	—	114	40	357
	31	—	12	—	262	35	—	194	57	716
III	527	148	4	4	17	—	—	417	—	1214
	980	254	4	5	26	—	—	636	—	2045
IV	7	32	1	13	28	—	—	327	—	613
	18	102	0	16	34	—	—	594	—	1082
V	5	211	1	0	1	—	—	—	—	298
	11	339	2	0	3	—	—	—	—	461

Table 43. Job content by major census industry, 1950 and 1960.
(thousands)

Public administration

	Tools		Mach. & equip.		Inspection	Vehicle operation	Farm	Sales A	Sales B
	spec.	nonspec.	spec.	nonspec.					
Total	24	299	14	70	85	48	—	9	3
	26	345	29	72	139	48	—	63	3
I	6	0	—	—	—	—	—	—	—
	8	0	—	—	—	—	—	—	—
II	2	69	10	—	22	2	—	6	—
	3	97	23	—	52	3	—	8	—
III	6	97	4	12	63	45	—	3	0
	7	118	6	14	88	44	—	54	0
IV	6	37	0	8	—	0	—	—	2
	4	41	0	6	0	0	—	—	3
V	4	96	—	50	0	0	—	—	0
	4	89	—	52	—	1	—	—	0

Public administration

	Clerical	Personal services	Enter-tainment	Protection	Admin. & org.	Research & design	Education	Health	Welfare	Total
Total	1130	49	2	338	249	87	8	14	42	2473
	1408	59	4	469	327	117	11	16	58	3194
I	49	—	2	—	40	76	8	5	42	229
	67	—	2	—	57	106	11	4	58	313
II	0	—	0	—	18	10	—	3	0	143
	0	—	0	—	37	11	—	3	0	239
III	892	10	0	291	191	—	—	5	—	1618
	1130	13	—	394	232	—	—	5	—	2104
IV	183	24	0	46	—	—	—	2	—	309
	207	27	0	58	—	—	—	4	—	351
V	5	15	0	1	0	—	—	—	—	174
	3	19	0	18	1	—	—	—	—	187

(*continued*)

BIBLIOGRAPHY

Books

ABRUZZI, ADAM. *Work, Workers, and Work Measurement.* New York: Columbia University Press, 1956.

BAKKE, E. WIGHT. *Labor Mobility and Economic Opportunity.* Cambridge, Massachusetts: Technology Press, 1954.

BELL, DANIEL. *Work and Its Discontents.* Boston: Beacon Press, 1956.

CAIRNES, J. E. *Some Leading Principles of Political Economy, Newly Expounded.* New York: Harper & Brothers, 1874.

CLARK, JOHN BATES. *Essentials of Economic Theory.* New York: Macmillan Co., 1927.

COMMONS, JOHN R. *Institutional Economics.* Madison: University of Wisconsin Press, 1959.

——— and associates. *History of Labour in the United States.* New York: Macmillan Co., 1918.

DUNLOP, JOHN T. *Industrial Relations Systems.* New York: Henry Holt & Co., 1958.

——— editor. *The Theory of Wage Determination.* London: Macmillan Co., 1957.

——— editor. *Automation and Technological Change.* Englewood Cliffs: Prentice-Hall, 1962.

EDWARDS, ALBA M. *Comparative Occupational Statistics for the United States, 1870–1940.* Washington: Bureau of the Census, 1943.

FRIEDMANN, GEORGES. *Industrial Society.* Glencoe, Illinois: The Free Press, 1955.

——— *The Anatomy of Work.* Glencoe, Illinois: The Free Press, 1961.

GEORGE, HENRY. *Social Problems.* Garden City: Doubleday, Page and Co., 1911.

HARBISON, FREDERICK H., and CHARLES A. MYERS. *Education, Manpower and Economic Growth.* New York: McGraw-Hill Book Co., Inc., 1964.

HERSKOVITS, MELVILLE J. *Economic Anthropology.* New York: Alfred A. Knopf, 1952.

JAFFE, A. J., and R. O. CARLETON. *Occupational Mobility in the United States, 1930–1960.* New York: King's Crown Press, 1954.

LESTER, RICHARD A. *Adjustments to Labor Shortages.* Princeton: Princeton University Press, 1955.

MALTHUS, T. R. *Principles of Political Economy.* New York: Augustus M. Kelly, 1951.

MARSHALL, ALFRED. *Principles of Economics.* London: Macmillan Co., 1936.

MARX, KARL. *Capital.* Chicago: Charles H. Kerr and Co., 1926.

MILL, JOHN STUART. *Principles of Political Economy*. London: Longsman, Green, and Co., 1929.

MILLER, HERMAN P. *Income of the American People*. New York: John Wiley & Sons, 1955.

NOSOW, SIGMUND, and WILLIAM H. FORM. *Man, Work, and Society*. New York: Basic Books, Inc., 1962.

PANCOAST, OMAR J. *Occupational Mobility*. New York: Columbia University Press, 1941.

RICARDO, DAVID. *Principles of Political Economy and Taxation*. London: George Bell and Sons, 1891.

ROE, ANNE. *The Psychology of Occupations*. New York: John Wiley & Sons, 1956.

SAY, JEAN-BAPTISTE. *A Treatise on Political Economy*. Philadelphia: John Grigg, 1827.

SHARTLE, CARROLL. *Occupational Information*. New York: Prentice-Hall, 1946.

SHILS, EDWARD B. *Automation and Industrial Relations*. New York: Holt, Rinehart, and Winston, 1963.

SMITH, ADAM. *The Wealth of Nations*. New York: Modern Library, 1937.

STIEBER, JACK. *The Steel Industry Wage Structure*. Cambridge, Massachusetts: Harvard University Press, 1959.

TAYLOR, FREDERICK W. *Scientific Management*. New York: Harper & Brothers, 1947.

TAYLOR, G. W., and F. C. PIERSON. *New Concepts in Wage Determination*. New York: McGraw-Hill Book Co., Inc., 1957.

TORRENS, ROBERT. *An Essay on the Production of Wealth*. London: Longman, Hurst, Rees, Orme, and Brown, 1821.

—— *On Wages and Combination*. London: Longman, Rees, Orme, Brown, Green, and Longman, 1834.

TUAN, MAO-LAN. *Simonde de Sismondi as an Economist*. New York: Columbia University Press, 1927.

U.S. DEPARTMENT OF LABOR, BUREAU OF EMPLOYMENT SECURITY. *Estimates of Worker Trait Requirements for 4000 Jobs*, 1956.

VENN, GRANT. *Man, Education and Work*. Washington: American Council on Education, 1964.

VERMEULEN, AD. *Job Evaluation in the Netherlands*. Paris: Organization for European Economic Cooperation, 1956.

WALKER, FRANCIS AMASA. *Discussions in Economics and Statistics*. New York: Henry Holt & Co., 1899.

—— *The Wages Question*. New York: Henry Holt & Co., 1886.

WRIGHT, CARROL D. *Outline of Practical Sociology*. New York: Longmans, Green, and Co., 1899.

Articles and Pamphlets

AARONSON, F. M., and R. A. KELLER. "Mobility of Workers in Employment covered by Old Age and Survivors Insurance." Social Security Administration, Bureau of Research and Statistics, Report 14, 1946.

ATKINSON, EDWARD. "Occupations in Their Relation to the Tariff," *Quarterly Journal of Economics*, XVII:2 (February 1903).

BERTILLON, JACQUES. "Classification of Occupations in the Census," *Journal of the American Statistical Association*, III:3 (September 1893).

BLAU, P. M., J. W. GUSTAD, R. JESSOR, H. S. PARNES, and R. C. WILCOCK. "Occupational Choice: A Conceptual Framework," *Industrial and Labor Relations Review*, IX:4 (July 1956).

BROZEN, YALE. "The Economics of Automation," *American Economic Review*, XLVII:2 (May 1957).

BUNTING, R. L. "A Test of the Theory of Geographical Mobility," *Industrial and Labor Relations Review*, XV:1 (October 1961).

CUMMINGS, JOHN. "Occupations in the Twelfth Census," *Journal of Political Economy*, XIII:1 (December 1904).

DANIEL, GORONWY H. "Some Factors Affecting the Movement of Labour," *Oxford Economic Papers* (February 1940).

DAVIS, LOUIS E. "The Effects of Automation on Job Design," *Industrial Relations*, II:1 (October 1962).

DUNLOP, JOHN T. "Estimates of Unemployment: Some Unresolved Problems," *Review of Economics and Statistics*, XXXII:1 (February 1950).

———— "Unemployment Statistics in a Changing Economy: One Academic View," *Proceedings of the American Statistical Association*, 1961.

ECKAUS, RICHARD S. "Economic Criteria for Education and Training," *Review of Economics and Statistics*, XLVI:2 (May 1964).

ECKERSON, A. B. "The New Dictionary of Occupational Titles," *Vocational Guidance Quarterly* (Autumn 1963).

EDWARDS, ALBA M. "Classification of Occupations," *Journal of the American Statistical Association*, XII:2 (June 1917).

———— "Social-Economic Groups in the United States," *Journal of the American Statistical Association*, XVII:2 (June 1917).

———— "A Social-Economic Grouping of the Gainful Workers of the United States," *Journal of the American Statistical Association*, XXVIII:4 (December 1933).

———— "The White Collar Worker," *Monthly Labor Review*, XXXVIII:3 (March 1934).

———— "The Negro as a Factor in the Nation's Labor Force," *Journal of the American Statistical Association*, XXXI:3 (September 1936).

—— "Growth and Significance of the White-Collar Class," *American Federationist*, XLV:1 (January 1938).

—— "Occupation and Industry Statistics," *Journal of the American Statistical Association*, XXXVI:3 (September 1941).

FINE, SIDNEY A. "Matching Job Requirements and Worker Qualifications," *Personnel* (May 1958).

—— "A Reexamination of 'Transferability of Skills'," *Monthly Labor Review* (August and September 1957).

GANNETT, HENRY. "The Classification of Occupations for Census Purposes," *Journal of the American Statistical Association*, IV:1–2 (March-June 1894).

HANSEN, ALVIN H. "Industrial Class Alignments in the United States," *Journal of the American Statistical Association*, XVII:4 (December 1920).

HOURWICH, ISAAC A. "The Social-Economic Classes of the Population of the United States," *Journal of Political Economy*, XIX:3–4 (March-April 1911).

HUNT, WILLIAM C. "Workers at Gainful Occupations at the Federal Censuses of 1870, 1880, and 1890," Department of Labor, Bulletin 11, July 1897.

—— "The Federal Census of Occupations," *Journal of the American Statistical Association*, XI:2 (June 1909).

KENDRICK, JOHN W. "Productivity Trends: Capital and Labor," *Review of Economics and Statistics*, XXXVIII:3 (August 1956).

KERR, CLARK, and ABRAHAM SIEGEL. "The Structure of the Labor Force in Industrial Society," *Industrial and Labor Relations Review*, VII:2 (January 1955).

KILLINGSWORTH, CHARLES C. "Automation in Manufacturing," *Industrial Relations Research Association*, XI.

LAMPMAN, ROBERT J. "New Facts and Interpretations in Labor Market Analysis," *Industrial and Labor Relations Review*, X:2 (January 1957).

LESTER, RICHARD A. "Labor Policy in a Changing World," *Industrial Relations*, II:1 (October 1962).

MAKOWER, H., J. MARSCHAK, and H. W. ROBINSON. "Studies in Mobility of Labor," *Oxford Economic Papers*, I (October 1938); II (May 1939); and IV (September 1940).

MANGUM, GARTH L. "Are Wage Incentives Becoming Obsolete?" *Industrial Relations*, II:1 (October 1962).

NATHAN, ROBERT R. "The Road to Full Employment," *Industrial Relations*, II:1 (October 1962).

NORTHRUP, HERBERT R. "Automation: Effects on Labor Force, Skills and Employment," *Industrial Relations Research Association*, XI.

OETTINGER, MARTIN P. "Nation-wide Job Evaluation in the Netherlands," *Industrial Relations*, IV:1 (October 1964).

PALMER, GLADYS L. "Some Considerations Involved in Appraising the Adequacy of Occupational Statistics," *Journal of the American Statistical Association*, XXXVI:1 (March 1941).

PHELPS, ORME W. "A Structural Model of the U.S. Labor Market," *Industrial and Labor Relations Review*, X:3 (April 1957).

PHELPS BROWN, E. H., and M. H. BROWNE. "Earnings in Industries of the United Kingdom, 1948–59," *Economic Journal*, LXXII:3 (September 1962).

RAIMON, ROBERT L. "Interstate Migration and Wage Theory," *Review of Economics and Statistics*, XLIV:4 (November 1962).

REDER, MELVIN. "The Theory of Occupational Wage Differentials,"*American Economic Review*, XLV:5 (December 1955).

ROBERTS, B. C. "National Wage Policy in the Netherlands," *Economica*, XXIV:3 (August 1957).

ROSS, ARTHUR M. "Do We Have a New Industrial Feudalism?" *American Economic Review*, XLVIII:5 (December 1958).

SCOVILLE, JAMES G. "The Development and Relevance of U.S. Occupational Data," *Industrial and Labor Relations Review*, XIX:1 (October 1965).

———— "Making Occupational Statistics More Relevant," Business and Economic Statistics Section, *Proceedings of the American Statistical Association, 1965.*

———— "Education and Training Requirements for Occupations," *Review of Economics and Statistics*, XLVIII:4 (November 1966).

———— "The Job Content of the Canadian Economy, 1941, 1951, and 1961," Dominion Bureau of Statistics (Ottawa), Special Labour Force Study No. 3, April 1967.

SOGGE, TILLMAN M. "Industrial Classes in the United States, 1870 to 1950," *Journal of the American Statistical Association*, XLIX:2 (June 1954).

SOLOW, ROBERT. "A Policy for Full Employment," *Industrial Relations*, II:1 (October 1962).

STEIN, HERBERT. "Reducing Unemployment: With or Without Inflation?" *Industrial Relations*, II:1 (October 1962).

STERN, JAMES. "Fact, Fallacy, and Fantasy of Automation," *Industrial Relations Research Association*, XI.

WHELPTON, P. K. "Occupational Groups in the United States, 1820–1920," *Journal of the American Statistical Association*, XXI:3 (September 1926).

ZOETEWEIJ, B. "National Wage Policy: The Experience of the Netherlands," *International Labour Review*, LXXI:2 (February 1955).

Unpublished Works

FINE, SIDNEY A. "The Nature of Automated Jobs and Their Educational and Training Requirements," an OMAT research document, Human Sciences Research, Inc., McLean, Virginia, 1965.

——— "The Use of Functional Job Analysis (FJA) to Predict Requirement Changes as a Result of Automation," an OMAT research document, Human Sciences Research, Inc., McLean, Virginia, 1964.

HANSEN, WILLIAM LEE. "Life Cycle Earnings Patterns and Intra-Occupational Differences in Earnings," unpub. diss., Johns Hopkins University, 1958.

HELLER, WALTER W. Statement before the Subcommittee on Employment and Manpower of the Senate Committee on Labor and Public Welfare, October 28, 1963.

OETTINGER, MARTIN P. "The Industrial Relations System in the Netherlands," unpub. diss., Harvard University, Cambridge, Massachusetts, 1960.

NOTES

Chapter 1

1. Adam Smith, *The Wealth of Nations* (New York: Modern Library, 1937), pp. 101, 127.

2. David Ricardo, *Principles of Political Economy and Taxation* (London: George Bell and Sons, 1891), pp. 383–384.

3. Karl Marx, *Capital* (Chicago: Charles H. Kerr and Co., 1926), pp. 406–415, 459–462, 478–487.

4. For a sketch of this history, see the author's article "The Development and Relevance of U.S. Occupational Data," *Industrial and Labor Relations Review*, 19:1 (October 1965), pp. 72–76.

5. *Comparative Occupational Statistics for the United States, 1870–1940* (Washington: U.S. Bureau of the Census, 1943), pp. xi, 175.

6. For further discussion, see the author's "Making Occupational Statistics More Relevant," Business and Economic Statistics Section, *Proceedings of the American Statistical Association*, 1965, pp. 317–319. Since these groups are, in principle, "social-economic," they should not be used for indicating skill levels, types of work, or homogeneous labor markets. Unfortunately, they are so employed all too frequently.

7. *Dictionary of Occupational Titles*, 1939, pp. xiii–xxvii.

8. Sidney A. Fine, "The Nature of Automated Jobs and Their Educational and Training Requirements," an OMAT research document, Human Sciences Research, Inc., McLean, Virginia, 1965, pp. 2, 34.

9. The concept of orientation has not been used in the *Dictionary*. For a criticism, see Scoville, "Making Occupational Statistics More Relevant," p. 322.

10. Fine, "The Nature of Automated Jobs," p. A-1. The assumptions and procedures are restated in the 1965 *Dictionary* in vol. I, p. xviii, and vol. iv, p. 649.

Chapter 2

1. An earlier classification by "foci" and "levels" was proposed by Anne Roe, *The Psychology of Occupations* (New York: John Wiley & Sons, 1956), Chap. 11. Neither dimension of her model is identical with the concepts proposed here, nor is this surprising in view of the differing orientations of psychology and economics. Dr. Roe's foci are sometimes close to the job families proposed below, but

some elements of job families enter into her levels as well. The reader may ponder the moral involved in the fact that she called my attention to her work after my own was well advanced.

2. John T. Dunlop, *Industrial Relations Systems* (New York: Henry Holt & Co., 1958), pp. 47ff.

3. John T. Dunlop, "The Task of Contemporary Wage Theory," in John T. Dunlop (ed.), *The Theory of Wage Determination* (London: Macmillan Co., 1957); E. R. Livernash, "The Internal Wage Structure," in G. W. Taylor and F. C. Pierson (eds.), *New Concepts in Wage Determination* (New York: McGraw-Hill Book Co., Inc., 1957). See also Peter B. Doeringer, "The Determinants of the Structure of Industrial Type Internal Labor Markets," *Industrial and Labor Relations Review*, January 1967.

4. Dunlop, "The Task of Contemporary Wage Theory," p. 16. The criterion of common wage-making characteristics appears in Appendix II as a test of the empirical experimentation here performed.

5. Livernash, "The Internal Wage Structure," p. 16.

6. Melvin Reder, "The Theory of Occupational Wage Differentials," *American Economic Review*, December 1955.

7. Wesley C. Mitchell, *Business Cycles*, part III, chap. 2, I:2.

8. Richard A. Lester, *Adjustments to Labor Shortages* (Princeton: Princeton University Press, 1955), pp. 22–25, 52–55.

9. Walter W. Heller, Statement before the Subcommittee on Employment and Manpower of the Senate Committee on Labor and Public Welfare, October 28, 1963.

10. For an earlier development of the tool-machine distinction and comments related to the concept of job family, see Max Weber, *The Theory of Social and Economic Organization* (Glencoe, Illinois: The Free Press of Glencoe, 1964), pp. 227–228.

11. *Census of Agriculture*, 1959, vol. II, pp. 1167–1172.

12. See Martin P. Oettinger, "The Industrial Relations System in the Netherlands," unpub. diss., Harvard University, 1960; and B. C. Roberts, "National Wage Policy in the Netherlands," *Economica*, August 1957.

13. International Labour Office, *Job Evaluation* (Geneva: I.L.O., 1960), p. 81, Appendix C, pp. 133–146.

14. United Steelworkers of America and United States Steel Corporation, *Job Description and Classification Manual*, January 1, 1953, pp. 9–10. For a discussion of the principles and development of this plan, see Jack Stieber, *The Steel Industry Wage Structure* (Cambridge, Mass.: Harvard University Press, 1959), chap.

II. The regression approach there described (pp. 33–35) is an interesting parallel to that employed in this study.

15. U.S. Department of Labor, Bureau of Employment Security, U.S. Employment Service, 1956. Since the time when the calculations were made, the third edition of the *D.O.T.* has been issued; its supplement of 1966 contains such information for jobs in the new *Dictionary*.

16. Richard S. Eckaus, "Economic Criteria for Education and Training," *Review of Economics and Statistics*, May 1964, pp. 184, 185n.

17. United States Department of Labor, Bureau of Employment Security, *Estimates of Worker Traits Requirements for 4000 Jobs* (Washington, 1956), p. v.

18. For a further discussion of this procedure, and an indication of some odd results, see the author's paper, "Education and Training Requirements for Occupations," *Review of Economics and Statistics*, November 1966.

Chapter 3

1. Grant Venn, *Man, Education and Work* (Washington: American Council on Education, 1964), p. 158.

2. Frederick H. Harbison and Charles A. Myers, *Education, Manpower and Economic Growth* (New York: McGraw-Hill Book Co., Inc., 1964), pp. 37–38.

3. Charles L. Schultze, *Recent Inflation in the United States*, a paper prepared for the Joint Economic Committee of the Congress of the United States, study paper no. 1, 1959. See in particular chap. 4.

4. Herman M. and Anne R. Somers, *Doctors, Patients and Health Insurance* (Washington: Brookings Institution, 1961), pp. 44–47.

5. The rank correlation coefficient between the nine pairs of observations is $-.10$. The standard error of r is $(n-1)^{-\frac{1}{2}}$, or .35.

Chapter 4

1. Outdoor Recreation Resources Review Commission, *Study Report 23*, Washington, D.C., 1962, p. 163.

Chapter 5

1. *Manpower Report of the President*, U.S. Department of Labor, March 1964, pp. 138, 253–254.

2. For many of these ideas, I am indebted to a discussion with Professor S. Kuznets. On this range of problems, reference can also be made to W. L. Hansen, "Life Cycle Earnings Patterns and Intra-Occupational Differences in Earnings," unpub. diss., Johns Hopkins University, 1958, especially Chap. I.

3. John T. Dunlop, Hearings before the Employment and Manpower Subcommittee of the Senate Committee on Labor and Public Welfare, 1963, pp. 303–304.

4. Richard S. Eckaus, "Economic Criteria for Education and Training," *Review of Economics and Statistics*, May 1964, pp. 184, 185n.

5. *Manpower Report of the President*, 1964, pp. 257–258.

PUBLICATIONS OF THE WERTHEIM COMMITTEE

Published by Harvard University Press

*HOUSER What the Employer Thinks, 1927
Wertheim Lectures on Industrial Relations, 1929
*HABER Industrial Relations in the Building Industry, 1930
*O'CONNOR Psychometrics, 1934
*NORGREN The Swedish Collective Bargaining System, 1941
BROWN Union Policies in the Leather Industry, 1947
*GALENSON Labor in Norway, 1949
DE SCHWEINITZ Labor and Management in a Common Enterprise, 1949
*ALTMAN Availability for Work: A Study in Unemployment Compensation, 1950
DUNLOP AND HILL The Wage Adjustment Board: Wartime Stabilization in the Building and Construction Industry, 1950
*GALENSON The Danish System of Labor Relations: A Study in Industrial Peace, 1952
FISHER The Harvest Labor Market in California, 1953
PURCELL The Worker Speaks His Mind on Company and Union, 1953
WHITE The New England Fishing Industry, 1954
LORWIN The French Labor Movement, 1954
TAFT The Structure and Government of Unions, 1954
BALDWIN Beyond Nationalization: The Labor Problems of British Coal, 1955
*WALKER Industrial Relations in Australia, 1956
MYERS Labor Problems in the Industrialization of India, 1958
*SPIRO The Politics of German Codetermination, 1958
LEISERSON Wages and Economic Control in Norway, 1945–1957, 1959
PEN The Wage Rate under Collective Bargaining, 1959
STIEBER The Steel Industry Wage Structure, 1959
PURCELL Blue Collar Man: Patterns of Dual Allegiance in Industry, 1960
KNOELLINGER Labor in Finland, 1960
SLICHTER Potentials of the American Economy: Selected Essays, edited by John T. Dunlop, 1961
CHRISTENSON Economic Redevelopment in Bituminous Coal, 1962
HOROWITZ The Italian Labor Movement, 1963
STURMTHAL Workers Councils: A Study of Workplace Organization on Both Sides of the Iron Curtain, 1964
JENSEN Hiring of Dock Workers and Employment Practices in the Ports of New York, Liverpool, London, Rotterdam, and Marseilles, 1964
BLACKMAN Presidential Seizure in Labor Disputes, 1967
INGBAR AND TAYLOR Hospital Costs in Massachusetts: An Econometric Study, 1968

Studies in Labor-Management History

ULMAN   The Rise of the National Trade Union: The Development and Significance of Its Structure, Governing Institutions, and Economic Policies, 1955

GOLDBERG   The Maritime Story: A Study in Labor-Management Relations, 1957, 1958

GALENSON   The CIO Challenge to the AFL: A History of the American Labor Movement, 1935–1941, 1960

HOROWITZ   The New York Hotel Industry: A Labor Relations Study, 1960

PERLMAN   The Machinists: A New Study in Trade Unionism, 1961

MUNSON   Labor Relations in the Lithographic Industry, 1953

MANGUM   The Operating Engineers: The Economic History of a Trade Union, 1964

BRODY   The Butcher Workmen: A Study of Unionization, 1964

MARSHALL   Labor in the South, 1967

TAFT   Politics American Style; The California Federation of Labor, 1968

Published by McGraw-Hill Book Company

ALEXANDER   Labor Relations in Argentina, Brazil, and Chile, 1962

STEVENS   Strategy and Collective Bargaining Negotiation, 1963

DUNLOP AND DIATCHENKO   Labor Productivity, 1964

SCOVILLE   The Job Content of the U.S. Economy, 1940–1970, 1969

DUNLOP AND FEDORENKO   Planning and Markets: Modern Trends in Various Economic Systems, 1969

* Out of Print.

INDEX